'It is no exaggeration to say that Ogden has pioneered a new pathway in psychoanalysis and has ingeniously created fresh paradigms without becoming mired in new orthodoxies. Instead, Ogden has consistently offered new perspectives: transitioning from a psychoanalysis that decodes to a psychoanalysis engaged in inventing, dreaming, and playing. In this book, Ogden continually shifts from a psychoanalysis that interprets to one that opens up fresh, surprising possibilities. His works read like stories. Personal experiences unfold and link in ways akin to dreams, tales, impossible puzzles, all of which stand in playful, creative relationships with one another.'

Antonino Ferro, *MD, recipient of the 2007 Sigourney Award and co-author of* The New Analyst's Guide to the Galaxy

'In lucid writing, Ogden illustrates the ways in which he works differently with each of his patients to create a form of psychoanalysis that facilitates the patient's making psychic changes required for him or her to become a fuller person. With his signature clarity of thinking, Ogden makes original contributions to analytic understandings of the unconscious, preverbal language, and unlived life. This book is a tour de force from which the reader is richly rewarded for the time he or she spends reading it.'

Glen O. Gabbard, *MD, Clinical Professor of Psychiatry at Baylor College of Medicine in Houston*

I0025071

What Alive Means

Internationally acclaimed for the clarity of his writing and thinking, Ogden radically reconceives psychoanalysis as a therapeutic process in which the patient is helped not only to achieve self-understanding, but to become more fully oneself.

The individual comes to experience life in a way that feels more real, more alive, more personal, more imaginative, and more one's own. Ogden is concerned with helping the patient reclaim lost life, life that one was not able to experience when it occurred because it was too painful, too confusing, and too dangerous. Ogden pushes the envelope of psychoanalysis as he presents ways in which he rethinks the concepts of the unconscious and analytic time. He expands on what it means to be oneself in an authentic way and how clinical process can help achieve that goal.

Building on Ogden's own highly influential work on the nature of psychoanalysis, this book is essential reading for all psychoanalysts and other readers interested in expanding their understanding of contemporary analytic thinking and clinical practice.

Thomas H. Ogden, MD, is the author of 13 books on the theory and practice of psychoanalysis, and three novels. His work has been translated into more than 25 languages. Ogden was awarded the Sigourney Award for his contributions to psychoanalysis in 2012. He practices and teaches psychoanalysis and creative writing in San Francisco, California.

What Alive Means

Psychoanalytic Explorations

Thomas H. Ogden

R Routledge
Taylor & Francis Group

LONDON AND NEW YORK

Designed cover image: Sandra Ogden

First published 2025
by Routledge
4 Park Square, Milton Park, Abingdon, Oxon, OX14 4RN

and by Routledge
605 Third Avenue, New York, NY 10158

Routledge is an imprint of the Taylor & Francis Group, an informa business

British Library Cataloguing-in-Publication Data
A catalogue record for this book is available from the British Library

Library of Congress Cataloging-in-Publication Data
Names: Ogden, Thomas H., author.
Title: What alive means: psychoanalytic explorations / Thomas H. Ogden.
Description: Abingdon, Oxon; New York, NY: Routledge, 2024. |
Includes bibliographical references and index. |
Identifiers: LCCN 2024037209 (print) | LCCN 2024037210 (ebook) |
ISBN 9781032867175 (hardback) | ISBN 9781032867168 (paperback) |
ISBN 9781003528821 (ebook)
Subjects: LCSH: Psychoanalysis.
Classification: LCC BF173 .O445 2024 (print) | LCC BF173 (ebook) |
DDC 150.19/5—dc23/eng/20241108
LC record available at https://lccn.loc.gov/2024037209
LC ebook record available at https://lccn.loc.gov/2024037210

ISBN: 9781032867175 (hbk)
ISBN: 9781032867168 (pbk)
ISBN: 9781003528821 (ebk)

DOI: 10.4324/9781003528821

Typeset in Optima LT Std
by codeMantra

Other books by Thomas H. Ogden

Nonfiction

Projective Identification and Psychotherapeutic Technique

The Matrix of the Mind: Object Relations and the Psychoanalytic Dialogue

The Primitive Edge of Experience

Subjects of Analysis

Reverie and Interpretation: Sensing Something Human

Conversations at the Frontier of Dreaming

This Art of Psychoanalysis: Dreaming Undreamt Dreams and Interrupted Cries

Rediscovering Psychoanalysis: Thinking and Dreaming, Learning and For-getting

On Not Being Able to Dream: Selected Essays, 1994–2005 (available only in Hebrew)

Creative Readings: Essays on Seminal Analytic Works

The Analyst's Ear and the Critic's Eye: Rethinking Psychoanalysis and Literature (co-authored with Benjamin Ogden)

Reclaiming Unlived Life: Experiences in Psychoanalysis

Coming to Life in the Consulting Room: Toward a New Analytic Sensibility

Fiction

The Parts Left Out: A Novel

The Hands of Gravity and Chance: A Novel

This Will Do…: A Novel

Aunt Birdie and Other Stories: A Collection of Short Stories

For Giuseppe Civitarese and Antonino Ferro

Contents

Introduction

Donald Winnicott and Wilfred Bion in the 1950s, 1960s, and 1970s initiated revolutionary change in the theory and practice of psychoanalysis. That revolution involved a transformation of psychoanalysis from what had been a discipline devoted to facilitating psychic change by means of enhancing self-understanding. In the hands of Winnicott and Bion, psychoanalysis has been transformed into a process in which experiences in analysis, jointly created by patient and analyst, enrich the patient's capacity to experience himself or herself as alive and real.

This shift in emphasis from understanding to experiencing does not involve a rejection of the value of self-understanding; rather, self-understanding becomes a powerful agent of psychic change when born of the patient's experiencing with the analyst something of what the patient has not previously been able to live. Critical to the psychic change that occurs as the patient reclaims unlived life is the patient's feeling of being recognized for who he is and who he is becoming.

The patient experiences unlived life not in the form of unconscious conflict, repressed urges or fantasies, but as a sense of emptiness and futility, a sense of not being present in one's own life. I think of this shift in balance from understanding to experiencing as a shift in emphasis from knowing and understanding (the epistemological dimension of psychoanalysis) to being and becoming (the ontological dimension of psychoanalysis). In the initial chapter of this book, I present my own way of working clinically in the ontological dimension of psychoanalysis.

This revolution in psychoanalysis initiated by Winnicott and Bion involves reconceiving many aspects of analytic theory. Winnicott, here, makes what is perhaps his most important contribution to psychoanalysis: his use of paradoxical thinking. Paradox underlies his groundbreaking concepts of transitional objects and phenomena, potential space, the experience of playing, the capacity to be alone, and creativity of every sort. I contribute to this intellectual movement as I present my own ways of rethinking the concepts of the unconscious and analytic time (Chapters 3 and 4).

Each of Winnicott's papers contributes something unique to the reworking of psychoanalysis. In the present volume, I offer creative readings of

DOI: 10.4324/9781003528821-1

four of Winnicott's watershed papers. In Chapters 2, 5, 7, and 8, I not only read Winnicott, I write Winnicott. When writing Winnicott, I am elaborating ideas that he suggests, but only suggests, and may not have been in his mind at all.

I then take up the theme of "what alive means" in relation to the transformations that occur at the dawn of verbal language (Chapter 8) at which time meaning is not transposed (from preverbal to verbal form); meaning is created. Entirely new cognitive experiences and feeling states come into being a qualitatively new form of living is born.

I close this book with a letter to a young writer in which I address the way in which we, in the act of writing in every genre, are not recording life; we are creating life.

1 Ontological psychoanalysis in clinical practice

I conceive of psychoanalysis as a therapeutic process involving two inter-dependent dimensions: the *ontological dimension*, which has to do with being and becoming, and the *epistemological dimension*, which has to do with coming to know and understand (Ogden, 2019, 2020). Just as the three dimensions of a material object are distinct and yet inseparable from one another, the epistemological and ontological dimensions of psychoanalysis do not exist in pure form. These dimensions stand in dialectical tension with one another: each creating, preserving, and negating the other, just as the conscious and unconscious mind create, preserve, and negate one another. (The concept of the unconscious mind is meaningless in the absence of the concept of the conscious mind. So too, the concept of ontological psychoanalysis is meaningless in the absence of the concept of epistemological psychoanalysis.)

The ontological dimension of psychoanalysis (coming into being) serves as the matrix within which the epistemological dimension (coming to understand) evolves. In other words, understanding is born of experiencing, but experiencing is not born of understanding. One may come into being in ways that do not involve self-understanding, for instance, in playing, dreaming, writing, and all other creative activities. Understanding oneself feels real only when born of experiencing.

As will be seen as I clinically illustrate the ontological dimension of psychoanalysis, I make little mention of object relations theory, which addresses the unconscious relationships among different aspects of oneself, a theory that is integral to my conception of analytic theory and practice. Nor do I mention reverie, which is a state of waking dreaming through which I gain a sense of what is occurring unconsciously in the analytic relationship (Ogden, 1994, 2004). These aspects of the way I think and work are not the focus of this chapter, though they are always critically important to the way I think and practice psychoanalysis. Neither is my focus the dialectic of conscious and unconscious mind. Rather, my interest here is on qualities of aliveness and deadness, realness and unrealness, the core of the self, the soul, if you will, all of which involve a way of being in the analytic setting different from searching for understanding of unconscious meaning (Ogden, 1995).

DOI: 10.4324/9781003528821-2

Epistemological and ontological dimensions of psychoanalysis

I view Freud and Klein as the principal architects of epistemological psychoanalysis and Winnicott and Bion as the principal architects of ontological psychoanalysis. Freud and Klein are predominantly interested in *the symbolic meaning* of dreams and children's play, while Winnicott and Bion are concerned primarily with *the experience* of playing and dreaming.

A methodology that characterizes epistemological psychoanalysis is the analyst's making verbal interpretations of the leading edge of anxiety in the transference; "Interpretation is at the heart of the Freudian doctrine and technique. Psychoanalysis itself might be defined in terms of it, as the bringing out of the latent meaning" (Laplanche & Pontalis, 1973, p. 227).

The analytic process, for both Freud and Klein, centrally involves making the unconscious conscious: "*Wo Es war, soll Ich werden*"/"Where id [it] was, there ego [I] shall be [or shall be becoming]" (Freud, 1933, p. 80[1]). Freud and Klein view the inner world as largely unconscious. Freud's (1900, 1933) interest is predominantly in the unconscious meaning of dreams, symptoms, associations, transference, and so on. Klein (1932, 1975) is predominantly interested in the meanings of unconscious phantasy as reflected, for instance, in children's play. But even here, the epistemological and ontological dimensions of psychoanalysis are inseparable. Freud's (1933) notion of the transformation of id into ego is at once a process of coming to understand the unconscious id (it) and a process of coming into being as ego (I).

For both Freud and Klein, the medium in which psychic change occurs is the process of making the repressed unconscious available to preconscious and conscious secondary process thinking and verbal symbolization. A principal goal of epistemological psychoanalysis is that of helping the patient achieve greater understanding of herself, particularly the repressed unconscious, thereby allowing the individual to experience herself and the external object world more realistically and with a greater range and depth of emotion.

Winnicott (1969a) comments on the limits of Freud's conception of psychoanalysis: "it is so difficult for us to believe that Freud has left us to carry on with the researches that his invention of psycho-analysis makes possible, and yet he cannot participate when we make a step forward" (p. 241).

Ontological psychoanalysis, as seen in the work of Winnicott and Bion, is principally concerned not with understanding the unconscious meanings of dreams and play but with playing and dreaming as growth-promoting living experiences that involve the entirety of the psyche-soma. Winnicott (1971a) concisely describes, in his own terms, the difference between the domains of what I call ontological and epistemological psychoanalysis:

> I suggest that in her writings Klein (1932), in so far as she was concerned with play, was concerned almost entirely with the use of play [as a form of symbolization of the child's inner world]. ... This is not a criticism of Melanie Klein or of others who have described the use of the child's play in the psychoanalysis of children. It is simply a comment on the

possibility that... the psychoanalyst has been too busy using play content to look at the playing child, and to write about playing as a thing in
itself. It is obvious that I am making a significant distinction between the
meanings of the noun "play" and the verbal noun "playing."

(pp. 39–40)

Here, Winnicott is locating a fundamental difference between epistemological and ontological psychoanalysis. The former is directed at nouns (the symbolic *use of play*), while ontological psychoanalysis is concerned with verbs
(the child's *playing*) in which the individual is experiencing the feeling of being alive and real, of coming to life, of becoming more oneself.

Ontological psychoanalysis places far less emphasis on the analyst's interpretations than does epistemological psychoanalysis. Winnicott (1969b)
comments:

It is only in recent years that I have become able to wait and wait for the
natural evolution of the transference arising out of the patient's growing
trust in the psychoanalytic technique and setting, and to avoid breaking
up this natural process by making interpretations.

(p. 86)

He continues this line of thought:

It appalls me to think how much deep change I have prevented or delayed... by my personal need to interpret. If only we can wait, the patient arrives at understanding creatively and with immense joy, and I
now enjoy this joy more than I used to enjoy the sense of having been
clever.

(p. 86)

The emphasis here is not on the content of what the patient learns from (his
understandings of) the analyst's interpretations. Rather, Winnicott's focus is on
the patient's processes of experiencing, the ways he "arrives at understanding
creatively and with immense joy," and not on the understanding at which the
patient arrives.

Winnicott (1969a) describes work with patients who are not able to be
present in their early experience because it was unbearable: "We now find
all these matters coming along for revival and correction in the transference
relationship, matters which are not so much for interpretation as for experiencing" (p. 242). Winnicott (1971b) makes this claim more broadly in saying,

the person we are trying to help might expect to feel cured when we
explain... In this kind of work we know that even the right explanation
is ineffectual. The person we are trying to help needs *a new experience*
in a specialized setting.

(p. 55, italics added)

And in still other words, he says, "madness that has to be remembered can only be remembered by reliving it" (Winnicott, 1965, p. 125).

A principal measure of psychic change in the ontological dimension of psychoanalysis lies in the degree to which the patient comes to experience his very being in a way that feels more fully alive and real, more fully himself. This may occur in the patient's experiencing qualities of being alive that range from the most primitive to the most mature. With regard to early trauma, Winnicott (1969a) is explicit about the limits of the role of understanding: "We now find all these matters coming along for revival and correction in the transference relationship, matters which are not so much for interpretation as for experiencing" (p. 242).

Critical to Winnicott's (1967) practice is his belief that experiences of being recognized by the analyst are pivotal to the analytic process:

> This glimpse of the baby's and the child's seeing the self in the mother's face, and afterwards in a mirror, gives a way of looking at analysis and at the psychotherapeutic task. Psychotherapy is not making clever and apt interpretations; by and large it is a long-term giving the patient back what the patient brings. It is a complex derivative of the face that reflects what is there to be seen. I like to think of my work this way, and to think that if I do this well enough the patient will find his or her own self, and will be able to exist and to feel real.
>
> (p. 117)

Bion's (1967a) contribution to the development of ontological psychoanalysis is reflected in his emphasis on the patient and analyst living together the unknown of the present moment of the analysis. The work of the analyst lies in his

> ... intuition of the reality [of what is occurring in the session] with which he must be at one. ...What is "known" about the patient is of no further consequence: it is either false or irrelevant. If it is "known" by patient and analyst, it is obsolete. ...The only point of importance in any session is the unknown. Nothing must be allowed to distract from intuiting that.
>
> (p. 136)

Bion, here, shifts the emphasis in psychoanalysis from the understanding of symbolic meaning to *intuiting* the reality "with which he must be at one." Being at one with reality, for both patient and analyst, is to experience the unfolding present moment of the analysis. In the work of intuiting, the analyst must resist the temptation to make use of memory and desire. Memory deals with what "is supposed to have happened" (Bion, 1967a, p. 136), and desire is concerned with "what has not yet happened" (p. 136). Memory and desire are distractions from the experience of being alive in the present moment of the session.

Bion's (1967b) view of interpretation is quite different from that of Freud and Klein:

> I think that what the patient is saying and what the interpretation is (which you give), is in a sense relatively unimportant. Because by the time you are able to give a patient an interpretation which the patient understands, all the work has been done.
>
> (p. 11)

In other words, by the time the analyst offers an interpretation of what is occurring in the session, the emotional (experiential) work associated with that understanding (which facilitates psychic change) has already occurred. Bion is also commenting here on how little he values what "the patient understands." In an analytic session, "understandings must not be allowed to proliferate" (Bion, 1967a, p. 137) for they subvert the patient's and the analyst's work of attending to the unknown. During his analysis with Bion, James Grotstein, in response to a comment made by Bion, said, "I understand." Bion impatiently replied, "If you must, circumstand, parastand, or metastand, but *please* try not to understand" (Grotstein, personal communication, 1983).

The principal project that runs through the entirety of Bion's opus involves a shift from the study of thoughts to the study of thinking. Bion's (1967a, 1967b, 1970) ideas on thinking ultimately took on a quintessentially ontological form in the concept of O (Civitarese, 2020), a notation that refers to the origin of everything: being, thinking, dreaming, intuiting, and so on. My understanding of O and K is that a reliance on K (the experience of coming to know) is of value only when it derives from O (the experience of the core of our being). We are fully alive when our knowing is derived from O. Being alive to oneself (O) cannot be derived from knowing (K); but coming to better know and understand (K) may arise from the experience of being alive and real to oneself (O). "The psycho-analytic vertex is O. With this the analyst cannot be identified: he must *be* it" (Bion, 1970, p. 27, italics in original). These conceptions of O and K underlie the idea that understanding is born of experiencing, while experiencing that feels real is not born of understanding.

Ferenczi's early contributions to the development of the ontological dimension of psychoanalysis, which began in 1925, are better appreciated when viewed from the perspective of the more fully elaborated understandings of Winnicott and Bion that I have discussed. Ferenczi (1932, 1949; Ferenczi & Rank, 1925) held that while Freud insufficiently appreciated the role of experience and overvalued understanding in the analytic process:

> The note of conviction is missing about knowledge acquired in any other way [other than by means of experiencing], no matter how compelling it may be in point of logic.
>
> (Ferenczi & Rank, 1925, p. 27)

The technique of interpretation is but one of the means of help in under-standing the unconscious mental condition of the patient, and not the aim, or certainly not the chief aim, of the analysis.

(Ferenczi & Rank, 1925, p. 29)

Thus we [Ferenczi and Rank] *finally come to the point of attributing the chief role in analytic technique to repetition* [experiencing in the analytic relationship] *instead of to remembering* [a cognitive, not an emotional phenomenon].

(1925, p. 4, italics in original)

In these passages, Ferenczi and Rank hold, as do Winnicott and Bion, that understanding (interpretation) in psychoanalysis may follow from experience, but experience does not follow from understanding.

In sum, when I use the term *the ontological dimension of psychoanalysis*, I am referring to a facet of the analytic process having to do with being and becoming more oneself. This evolution of self occurs in the medium of experiences in the analytic setting in which the patient is recognized by the analyst in a way that feels real to the patient. The use of a *technique* (a way of practicing psychoanalysis developed by a branch of one's analytic ancestry) is antithetical to ontological psychoanalysis in that an agreed-upon methodology limits spontaneity, which is critical to work in the ontological dimension of the analytic process. I prefer to use the term *style* to refer to the way the analyst has developed his or her own way of being an analyst (Ogden, 2007).

Clinical illustrations

I will now offer clinical illustrations of the ontological dimension of psychoanalysis in clinical practice. Each situation I shall describe is specific to a moment in analysis created by a particular analyst and a particular patient and would not occur in an analysis conducted by any other analytic pair. Each analyst with each patient must together *reinvent psychoanalysis* (Ogden, 2018, p. 57).

Do I have to draw you a picture?

When I met her in the waiting room for our first meeting, Ms. L appeared to be in her mid- to late twenties. She was sitting in a chair reading a magazine, which she continued listlessly to read before looking up at me. As I stood there, I felt as if our roles had been reversed: I was waiting to see her. She lifted her head and looked wearily in my direction as if I were a hotel valet delivering a written message.

Once we were seated in my consulting room, I looked at Ms. L in a way that invited her to begin. She looked expectantly at me.

I said after a bit of silence, "Where should we begin?"

She looked at me and said, "I guess I'm supposed to tell you why I've come to see you, what my parents are like, what happened in my childhood. That's the way things work, don't they?"

"I don't know how things work."

"Don't play games with me."

"I don't play games."

"I've been in therapy before. I know you have a way of doing things, so why don't you just tell me what it is."

"I just talk with the person I'm with and see what happens."

"You ask questions, I give answers. Right?"

"I've never thought of it that way."

Scoffing, she turned her head to survey my consulting room. "This is a pretty small place in the basement of a house. Your house?"

"It's where I work."

Ms. L said, "You probably think you're very smart and know how to establish your authority. Is that what you're doing?"

"I get the feeling that you wouldn't mind what I'm up to so long as you understand what it is."

"Yes, that's what I just told you. Do I have to draw you a picture?"

"Would you?"

"Would I what?"

"Draw me a picture."

"Are you serious?"

"I am."

"You have crayons and a coloring book?" she said, seeming curious about this development.

"No, just a pad of paper and a pen or pencil." I rummaged through the contents of the basket next to my chair looking for a pencil or pen and the spiral notebook I keep there. I leaned forward in my chair offering her the notebook and pencil.

She asked, "What are you doing?" as she took the pad and pencil from me.

"I'm inviting you to draw me a picture."

"I have nothing to draw."

"Well, that may be your first drawing. A blank page."

"No, I don't want to draw anything," she said, holding the pad and pencil tightly to her chest, as if I might try to take them away from her.

"That's all right. I like the first drawing."

"What are you talking about?"

"The blank page is like the title page of a book. I'd be intrigued by a book with a blank title page."

"You're talking rubbish."

"I mean what I'm saying."

"This is a waste of time. . . I did well in school, had friends. In junior high, I couldn't concentrate or stay still in class, they put me in a class for dumb kids where I was bored out of my mind. I felt like I was in a cell without windows or doors."

"Time was endless and the place inescapable."

"That's right." After a very brief pause, she said, "Aren't you going to say something more?"

"I'm thinking."

"What are you thinking?"

"Can't I have any privacy?"

"What are you up to?"

Ms. L placed the notebook on the upper knee of her crossed legs and began to draw. Something in what she drew seemed to catch her interest, which led her to draw a little bit more before tearing the page out of the notebook, crumpling it, and throwing it to the floor next to her.

I said, "Drawing's a very difficult thing to do."

She said quietly, "I don't have anything to draw." She picked up the pad from her knee and again held it tightly to her chest, with her arms crossed over the pad, each hand reaching for the opposite shoulder.

I said, "You began to draw something, but you stopped. I imagine that you feel like that a lot."

"All the time," Ms. L responded.

"Even though it's a terrible feeling, it is real."

"What good does that do me?"

"It's a beginning, even though it doesn't feel that way."

She began to cry. "You're really getting me upset now. I don't need congratulations on having nothing to draw."

"You tried to draw when you felt you had nothing to draw."

"I don't see what good came of it."

"Perhaps you were telling me something about why you've come to see me."

Ms. L was quiet for a while before saying, "Maybe."

In this exchange, Ms. L experienced with me her inarticulate wish to create something that reflected who she was and what she wanted from the work with me, as well as the collapse of that process in its early stages. She was incapable of describing these feeling states in words, so the communication had to be achieved in the form of a series of experiences with me.

I was surprised by much of what I was spontaneously saying and doing with Ms. L, while at the same time feeling that I was creating a form of psychoanalysis for her that seemed new, yet familiar, to me. For much of the session I felt as if I were being carried by the force of an emotional process in which Ms. L and I were creating something together for which neither of us had words. We were making what Seamus Heaney (1978) calls a "raid [on] the inarticulate" (p. 47)—inarticulate meaning coming into being in experience before becoming meaning of a sort that can be known and spoken and understood.

The ontological aspect of psychoanalysis, the aspect having to do with coming into being, was primary in the portion of the session I have described. Ms. L was initially not able to speak to herself, much less to me, about how difficult it was for her to experience herself as real and alive, a person capable of coming to life in a creative way that felt like her own. The communication concerning these matters occurred in the experiences that unfolded in the session. They were experiences in which Ms. L was not able to reduce me to preconceived patterns, experiences in which Ms. L felt unable to draw (to create herself, to come into her own), but nonetheless tried to do so. Toward the end of the exchange, I offered Ms. L a tentative understanding of what had occurred between us. These experiences served as the groundwork upon which self-understanding took root, a partial understanding of why she came to see me: "Perhaps you were telling me something about why you've come to see me." To which, the patient responded, "Maybe." The entirety of the experience that preceded was necessary for the understanding to feel real to the patient and to me.

You don't know the half of it

Ms. N, a woman in her late fifties, came to her first meeting skeptical of me and of analysis. She said she did not like seeing a psychiatrist because she was not stupid; she knew that psychiatrists are trained to prescribe medications and not for talking with patients. She said:

> I've been told that you write but that does not interest me because I know that psychiatrists write just to see themselves in print, an exercise in vanity. I have to be honest with you, I know that the fees therapists are charging are outrageous, and psychiatrists charge more than anyone else.

As the session went on, she added:

> If I'm going to be completely honest with you, I find your cold windowless waiting room to be an insult to patients. I could see before even meeting you that you don't give much thought to that sort of thing.

It was hard for me to take these criticisms seriously. Her tone of voice, the rhythm of her speech, and the expression on her face led me to feel that the patient was not taking what she said seriously either.

I replied to her criticisms, "You don't know the half of it."

"Go on. You're not serious... are you?"

"Entirely serious."

"Go on..."

Until that point in the session, Ms. N had not quite been looking me in the eye; her gaze went through me as if looking at someone behind me. At this point in the session, her eyes met mine and a slight smile that felt genuine flickered across her face.

In this exchange, I did not respond to the patient with either silence or a question or a bit of understanding concerning feelings that may arise in an initial analytic consultation, such as "Meeting with me must feel like a dangerous thing to do." Instead, my comment, "You don't know the half of it," was a response to a hint of playfulness and humor that I heard in Ms. N's voice and facial expressions which I took as an invitation to play with the caricature she was drawing of me. Her meeting my eyes with hers and her fleeting smile in response to my saying, "You don't know the half of it," felt alive to me and a good footing with which to begin an analysis.

The humor in my comment was a form of playing. Only later, as I thought about it, did I recognize that I had been commenting on the situation that exists at the outset of every analysis. The patient does not know the half of what is happening, nor do I concerning why the patient has come for analysis, what it will feel like to engage in the analysis, who will the patient and I become as the analysis proceeds, and innumerable other questions.

The moment in the analysis I have described is ontological in nature in that it is all about who the patient was and was becoming, and it was mediated not by understandings but by lived experience in which the patient saw herself reflected in me, recognized by me.

There you are

I met Alex when he was admitted to a long-term analytically oriented inpatient ward for adolescents where I was a staff psychiatrist. Alex was nineteen years old, short and thin, his face expressionless. He had had a psychotic breakdown with auditory hallucinations and paranoia. He spoke in words impossible to understand. He had, from the time he was four or five, had great difficulty with social relationships, even with his parents. He mostly kept to himself in his room. On being admitted to the ward, he hid under the covers of his bed.

I will focus on a particular moment in our work together. Alex and I met five times a week, at first for short periods of time. In the initial months, the sessions were mostly silent, his eyes fixed on the floor. Occasionally, I told Alex what I felt like as I sat with him. As he began to talk, he spoke in a soft, high-pitched voice that seemed otherworldly; what he said seemed to be moving in the direction of a declarative statement or question but trailed off into incoherence. As the months went by, he spoke in sentences that were comprehensible but almost completely devoid of feeling, which gave his speech a bland, monotonous quality.

About eight months into our work, Alex told me in his usual bland way that his father had come to visit the previous day. "God he's ugly."

I replied, "Did you get the name of the guy who just said that?" Alex, surprised by my question, uncharacteristically raised his gaze from the floor to look at me. This moment in our work remains with me decades later because it marked a step in his beginning to open himself to me. The ontological dimension of this moment involved my recognizing Alex as he was beginning to dare to come into his own as a person with thoughts and feelings. In saying, "Did you get the name of the guy who just said that?" I was in effect saying to him, "There you are" in a way that reflected the fleeting quality of his coming into his own with me.

Bag lunches

Mr. W was a man in his late fifties when he came to see Dr. M, an analytic colleague of mine. He told Dr. M that he had in the past consulted two analysts but had found it difficult to tolerate the "power differential" between him and the analyst and had walked out of his first session on the couch. Mr. W told Dr. M he had been married for 30 years and had two grown children. Mr. W seemed fragile, so Dr. M did not press him to say more about anything he said.

At the end of their first meeting, Dr. M said, "Let's not do analysis. Why don't we just have lunch together; we'll bring bag lunches."

They each brought a bag lunch and talked about anything Mr. W wanted to talk about. He loved art and would tell Dr. M about art exhibits at the local museums and at museums around the country and around the world. He said he and his wife were at their best together at art galleries and museums. She admired his knowledge and taste in art. Dr. M understood what he said about art to be Mr. W's way of speaking about his inner world and the relationships with people who were important to him, but the analyst did not make comments connecting the two realms.

They met once a week for many years. When the weather was good, they sat on a bench in the park. When it rained or was too cold, they sat in the two armchairs in the analyst's consulting room. It was not until they had met for some years that Mr. W began to talk with Dr. M about his current life and his life as a child. He said he was prone to outbursts of anger that frightened his wife and his children, and frightened him as well. It took considerably longer for him to tell the analyst about his older brother's bullying him and his feeling that he was a weakling and not sufficiently masculine, which continued to this day. Dr. M let the patient take the lead at every turn in their work together. The patient cried as he spoke about his having hit his older son when he was very young and his wish that he could undo it. He was then able to talk with his son about his regret that he had behaved in that way.

To my mind, it was the fact that Dr. M invented a form of psychoanalysis that Mr. W was able to use that was most important and most generative for this patient. Understandings followed but could not have occurred in the absence of the experience.

Creating analysis for, and with, Mr. W represented the ontological dimension of psychoanalysis in which the analyst recognized who the patient was and adjusted to him in a way that fostered the patient's coming into being. Understandings concerning the patient's feeling weak and insufficiently masculine came later but were inextricably intertwined with the experience of being recognized and accepted by the analyst.

I was, and continue to be, greatly admiring of the analysis Dr. M created with this patient. I think of it often. It is an analysis I could not have created myself.

I wish I could but must accept the fact that no two analysts create analyses with their patients in the same way.

A call in the evening

Mr. V said he came for analysis "to learn more about myself," a vague statement that seemed to me to reflect a feeling that he was either holding secrets or not sufficiently a person to have problems with which to wrestle. It took some months of analysis before he dropped hints regarding the fact that he had been sleeping in the same bed with his ten-year-old daughter for more than a year while his wife slept alone in their bedroom. He paid lip service to being aware that there were problems in this arrangement for both his daughter and his wife. He treated me as if I were his friend, not his analyst, thus attempting to obscure role difference (and symbolic generational difference) between the two of us. I directed him to stop sleeping with his daughter. He subsequently told me he had done so, but I did not trust that he had.

I received a phone call from Mr. V late one evening. "We've got a problem. I'm in a police station. I've been arrested for drunk driving."

I replied without planning, "We don't have a problem, you have a problem."

He was speechless, and then sardonically replied, "Thanks for all your help, Doctor."

In saying what I did to Mr. V, I was spontaneously creating with him an experience that might have an impact far greater than making an interpretive comment such as "You don't like it when you find there are laws you haven't written." In the brief interchange with Mr. V, I was confronting him with the reality of the role difference and generational difference between him and me, and between him and his daughter, as well as the fact that he does not write the laws he is subject to.

The structure of the family in which Mr. V grew up was one in which generational difference was blurred. He told me he was instructed to look after his alcoholic mother while his father disowned any responsibility for the family. The patient, as a child, had been conscripted into a form of pseudo-adulthood he could not manage. It seemed to me that Mr. V had unconsciously gone into analysis with me in hopes of dealing with the ways in which his confusion regarding generational difference and the law of the father, as Lacan calls it, were reflected in his creating an incestuous relationship with his daughter, which seemed to excite him as much as it repelled him.

The intervention I made during the phone call reflected the ontological dimension of the analysis as it was unfolding at that moment. I was telling him that I was not at one with him in the problem he had created for himself by breaking the law. I was drawing a line, marking the difference between the two of us regarding his lack of adherence to laws prohibiting incestuous relationships with children and generational difference between the two of us. Understandings were of no value to this man at the moment I am describing. Communication had to occur in the medium of the experiences we created with one another.

Rats in a metal cage

Mr. T, a man in his thirties, came to his Monday session in the fourth year of analysis looking blanched. His voice trembled as he told me that there were rats in his house. He already had a man from a pest control company set traps and plug holes at points where the man believed the rats had found entry into the house. Despite the traps and other measures, Mr. T could hear the rats scurrying in the ceiling and walls of his bedroom. He spoke in a highly pressured way as he attempted to tell me the whole story at once. He said, "I'm frightened that the rats will get into my bed while I'm sleeping and bite me. It's like the rats in the metal facemask in *1984*."

I said to him, "You're not frightened, you're terrified."

When I said this to Mr. T, he calmed and was quiet for a bit. My comment could be labeled empathic or understanding, but I did not experience it that way. It reflected my recognition of who the patient was at that moment. My recognizing him conveyed the fact that I knew him at a depth; consequently, he was not alone.

I am mentioning this moment in the analysis because it so centrally involves recognizing who the patient was at a critical moment in the analysis. Being frightened is a state in which something is felt to be dangerous and threatening; being terrified is a state of being stricken, paralyzed, as helpless as an infant, facing imminent rape of the core of the self. My statement was ontological in the sense that his feeling recognized was what was of most value to him; it rendered him less alone.

Concluding comment

In the clinical illustrations I have presented, the process of the patient's (and the analyst's) coming more fully into being occurred in the medium of experiences in which the patient felt recognized at a depth by the analyst for the individual he or she was and was becoming. This type of experience took place in the context of analyses in which patient and analyst were creating together an analysis only the two of them could have created. The analyst was not practicing a technique; he was being himself as an analyst, making use of a style he had developed, and was being spontaneous in his work. All of this taken together constitutes the ontological dimension of psychoanalysis.

Note

1 Freud (1926) asked that *das Is* and *das Ech* be translated as "simple pronouns" ("das Es and das Ich," *the I and the it*) to describe our two agencies or provinces instead of giving them orotund Greek names (p. 195).

References

Bion, W. R. (1967a). Notes on memory and desire. In *Wilfred Bion: Los Angeles Seminars and Supervision*, ed. J. Aguayo & B. Malin. London: Karnac, 2013, pp. 136–138.

Bion, W. R. (1967b). First seminar: 12 April 1967. In *Wilfred Bion: Los Angeles Seminars and Supervision*, ed. J. Aguayo & B. Malin. London: Karnac, 2013, pp. 1–31.

Bion, W. R. (1970). *Attention and Interpretation*. London: Tavistock.

Civitarese, G. (2020). The limits of interpretation. A reading of Bion's "On Arrogance." *Int. J. Psychoanal.* 82: 236–257.

Ferenczi, S. (1932). The Clinical Diary of Sandor Ferenczi, ed. J. Dupont, trans. M. Balint & N. Jackson. Cambridge, MA: Harvard University Press, 1995.

Ferenczi, S. (1949). Confusion of the tongues between the adults and the child (The language of tenderness and of passion). *Int. J. Psychoanal.*, 30: 225–230.

Ferenczi, S. & Rank, O. (1925). *The Development of Psycho-Analysis*. Mansfield Center, CT: Martino Fine Books, 2012.

Freud, S. (1900). The Interpretation of Dreams. *S. E.*, 4–5. London: Hogarth Press.

Freud, S. (1926). The Question of Lay Analysis: Conversations with an Impartial Person. *S. E.*, 20. London: Hogarth Press.

Freud, S. (1933). *New Introductory Lectures on Psychoanalysis. S. E.*, 22. London: Hogarth Press.

Heaney, S. (1978). *Preoccupations: Selected Prose, 1968–1978*. London: Farrar Straus, p. 47.

Klein, M. (1932). *The Psychoanalysis of Children*. London: Hogarth Press, 1949.

Klein, M. (1975). *Envy and Gratitude and Other Works, 1946–1963*. New York: Delacorte Press/Seymour Laurence.

Laplanche, J. & Pontalis, J.-B. (1973). *The Language of Psycho-Analysis*. New York: Norton.

Ogden, T. H. (1994). The analytic third – Working with intersubjective clinical facts. *Int. J. Psychoanal.* 75: 3–20.

Ogden, T. H. (1995). Analysing forms of aliveness and deadness of the transference-countertransference. *Int. J. Psychoanal.* 76: 695–710.

Ogden, T. H. (2004). This art of psychoanalysis: dreaming undreamt dreams and interrupted cries. *Int. J. Psychoanal.* 85: 857–878.

Ogden, T. H. (2007). Elements of analytic style: Bion's clinical seminars. *Int. J. Psychoanal.*, 88: 1185–1200.

Ogden, T. H. (2018). How I talk with my patients. *Psychoanal. Q.* 87: 399–414.

Ogden, T. H. (2019). Ontological psychoanalysis or "What do you want to be when you grow up?" *Psychoanal. Q.* 88: 661–684.

Ogden, T. H. (2020). Toward a revised form of analytic thinking and practice: the evolution of analytic theory of mind. *Psychoanal. Q.* 89: 219–243.

Winnicott, D. W. (1965). The psychology of madness: a contribution from psychoanalysis. In *Psycho-analytic Explorations*, ed. C. Winnicott, R. Shepherd & M. Davis. London: Karnac Books, 1989, pp. 119–129.

Winnicott, D. W. (1967). Mirror-role of mother and family in child development. In *Playing and Reality*. New York: Basic Books, pp. 111–118.

Winnicott, D. W. (1969a). The use of an object in the context of Moses and Monotheism. In *Psycho-Analytic Explorations,* ed. C. Winnicott, R. Shepherd & M. Davis. London: Karnac Books, 1989, pp. 240–243.

Winnicott, D. W. (1969b). The use of an object and relating through identifications. In *Playing and Reality*. New York: Basic Books, pp. 86–94.

Winnicott, D. W. (1971a). Transitional objects and transitional phenomena. In *Playing and Reality*. New York: Basic Books, pp. 1–25.

Winnicott, D. W. (1971b). Playing: creative activity and the search for the self. In *Playing and Reality*. New York: Basic Books, pp. 53–64.

2 What alive means

On Winnicott's "Transitional objects and transitional phenomena"

Winnicott (1971a) takes on a most difficult task in "Transitional objects and transitional phenomena": that of describing the origins of the feeling of being alive, a state of being that Winnicott believes has its roots in the early life of the infant and continues throughout the life of the individual. This state of being, the experience of feeling alive, was a neglected subject in psychoanalysis prior to Winnicott's publication of this paper, and this paper, 70 years after it was first delivered, remains one of the most important papers in the analytic literature.

I will offer a reading of Winnicott's (1971a) "Transitional objects and transitional phenomena" in three parts: the first focuses on theory and the second on the new clinical material Winnicott adds to the final version of his paper (1971a). The third part of this chapter is devoted to a discussion of a fragment of an analysis I conducted in which a radical alteration of the analytic frame played an important role in the patient's beginning to experience his feelings as real.

The intermediate space

"Transitional objects and transitional phenomena" was originally delivered to the British Psychoanalytical Society in 1951; in 1953 Winnicott published a revised version of the paper in the *International Journal of Psychoanalysis*, a further revised version was published in *Through Paediatrics to Psychoanalysis* (1958a), and the final version of the paper was published in *Playing and Reality* (1971b), the year of Winnicott's death. (All references in this chapter, unless otherwise indicated, will be to the final version: 1971a.)[1]

It seems to me that Winnicott, throughout this paper, is speaking to Freud and Klein, a bit wary of the reception his new conceptualization of human experiencing will receive.

Near the beginning of the paper, Winnicott states:

> I have introduced the terms "transitional objects" and "transitional phenomena" for designation of the intermediate area of experience, between the thumb and the teddy bear, between the oral erotism and the true

DOI: 10.4324/9781003528821-3

object-relationship, between primary creative activity and projection of what has already been introjected, between primary unawareness of indebtedness and the acknowledgement of indebtedness ("Say: 'ta'").

(p. 2)

In a single sentence, Winnicott illustrates four ways of describing an "intermediate area of experience," each of which derives from already established lines of developmental thinking fundamental to the work of both Freud and Klein. What is new here is Winnicott's locating the infant's experience of transitional objects and transitional phenomena *between* each of theses four sets of developmental stages. In so doing, he is beginning to create a new analytic conception not only of development but of experiencing itself, which is created in *the space between* the already familiar developmental landmarks.

The idea of "the space between" is pivotal to Winnicott as an analytic theorist throughout his opus, for example, the intermediate space between what has already happened and what the patient fears is going to happen (Winnicott, 1974); "*the potential space...* that exists (but cannot exist)" between mother and infant (Winnicott, 1971c, p. 107); the intermediate area between the mother's being destroyed and her surviving destruction by the infant (Winnicott, 1969); the space between the infant's being alone and his being in his mother's presence (Winnicott, 1958b). For Winnicott, the space between one and two is not one-and-a-quarter or one-and-a-half or some other numerical fractional, but the place in which a different order of experiencing, at once real and illusory, is created. If the new order of experience is not emergent from the intermediate area, the individual is not coming to life (Ogden, 1995).

Winnicott describes some of the infant's or child's early forms of transitional phenomena:

By this definition an infant's babbling and the way an older child goes over a repertory of songs and tunes while preparing for sleep come within the intermediate area as transitional phenomena.

(p. 2)

While much had been written about the infant's progress "from 'hand to mouth' to 'hand to genital'" (p. 3) activity, far less had been written about the infant's movement to the healthy handling of "truly 'not-me' objects" (p. 3) and the tendency "to weave other-than-me objects into the personal pattern" (p. 3). I find quite remarkable the wording here: "to weave other-than-me objects into the personal pattern." So much is conveyed here about the texture of the experience of transitional objects: *they are very early encounters with what is not-me, and yet they are being woven into what is absolutely personal to an infant who is early in the process of becoming a subject.* The infant, with the help of the mother, arrives at a solution to the problem of how to maintain the delicate balance involved in coming to life as a distinct individual:

his creation of a transitional object "in the intermediate area between the subjective and that which is objectively perceived" (p. 3). Though the infant may seem to create transitional objects on his own, he or she is able to do so only because "The mother places the actual breast just there where the infant is ready to create, and at the right moment" (p. 11).

Relating to transitional objects involves "some abrogation of omnipotence" (p. 5); that is, the object is not entirely experienced by the infant as his creation. The transitional object is resilient, "affectionately cuddled as well as excitedly loved and mutilated" (p. 5). It must seem to the infant "to give warmth, or to move... or do something that seems to show it has vitality or reality of its own" (p. 5). It is essential that it feel to the infant like a "not-me possession" (p. 1)—mine, but not me. "[T]he pattern of transitional phenomena begins to show at about six to eight to twelve months" (p. 4).

"The point of it [the transitional object] is not its symbolic value so much as its actuality" (p. 6). The relationship with the transitional object is an experience of an object that exists as a tangible object and holds meaning in its own right aside from what symbolic value it might hold.

Often the term *transitional object* is used to refer to an object that serves to help the child make the transition from relating to subjective objects (largely projections of the child's inner world) to relating to objects objectively perceived. This is true, but it is far too limited a conception of transitional objects. It seems to me that what Winnicott has in mind when he speaks of transitional objects and phenomena is antithetical to developmental thinking, which is intrinsically linear and chronological in nature. Winnicott's way of conceiving of "the intermediate space" rejects cause-and-effect, chronological, and binary thinking. He insists that psychoanalytic thinking require something qualitatively different from a two-part conception of human experiencing that involves: (1) one's engagement with "interpersonal relationships [including]... the whole of fantasy... [and] the repressed unconscious" (p. 2) and (2) one's involvement with one's *"inner reality"* (p. 2).

> My claim is that if there is a need for this double statement, there is also need for a triple one, the third part of the life of a human being, a part that we cannot ignore, is an intermediate area of *experiencing,* to which inner reality and external life both contribute.
>
> (p. 2)

Though transitional objects and phenomena do contribute to the maturation of the individual, they are not simply parts of a developmental process. They constitute a form of experiencing that remains long after self-object differentiation has been achieved. Transitional objects and phenomena are an aspect of the "journey of the progress towards experiencing" (p. 6), a part of the evolution of experiencing itself. They are "the place where we live" (Winnicott, 1971c), the *place where we are alive* to our experience of ourselves and the world.

The verb form ("experiencing" as opposed to "experience") is critical to Winnicott's thinking because this "third part" of the triple statement of psychic and somatic life is always in movement, always on the wing, and always in the process of change. It is an area of experiencing that is

> not challenged, because no claim is made on its behalf except that it shall exist as a resting-place for the individual engaged in the perpetual human task of keeping inner and outer reality separate yet interrelated.
>
> (p. 2)

There, in the intermediate area of experiencing, is "a resting-place" in which neither the inner world nor the outer world is "making a claim" on the infant, where the infant is not "challenged" by either external or internal reality regarding the question: Is what you are experiencing fantasy or reality?

Part of what is wondrous to me about this early portion of Winnicott's paper is that the revolution in the analytic understanding of human experiencing that Winnicott is introducing is grounded in what has been fully apparent to everyone who has spent time with an infant or child and witnessed the phenomenon of an infant babbling to himself; a child singing songs or inventing tunes when no one else is listening; the great importance of the attachment of children to the satin edges of their blankets or to a particular silken piece of fabric; or a child or group of children playing "seriously," that is, with fullest emotional engagement and concentration. But it is not until Winnicott's delivery of the first version of this paper in 1951 that these quotidian phenomena came to serve as the basis for a restructuring of our understanding of fundamental qualities of all human experiencing: feelings of aliveness and deadness, realness and unrealness, truthfulness and untruthfulness.

Winnicott states what he finds to be common to the experience of transitional objects in still another way:

> Of the transitional object it can be said that it is a matter of agreement between us and the baby that we will never ask the question: "Did you conceive of this or was it presented to you from without?" The important point is that no decision on this point is expected. The question is not to be formulated.
>
> (p. 12)

Here Winnicott is locating the creation of transitional objects in the area where the infant simultaneously conceives of (imagines) the object and has it presented to him (where he "discovers" the object by objectively perceiving it), and there is "agreement" between adults and infants never to ask whether the infant has created or discovered the object. This formulation of transitional objects has in the past provided me a feeling that I finally understand the meaning of the terms "transitional objects" and "transitional phenomena." But, now, as I read this passage, I find it to be too clear. The weakness of these sentences, for me, is that they are explanatory. The words tell us that by agree-ment between parents and the infant, the infant is not to be asked if he or she is creating or discovering the object. The question is not formulated—it does not even occur to the parents or infant to ask the question. But these concepts do not provide me with a sense of what is occurring, for example, during my experience of writing this paper, during which clock time disappears, and in its place is "dream time" and "dream space," and an experience of myself that feels decidedly different from the way I experience myself in most other parts of my life. The in-between space "that belongs to the arts and to religion and to imaginative living, and to creative scientific work" (p. 14) remains an enigma to me, impossible to penetrate—not reducible to the terms of creat-ing/discovering/not questioning—and remains a domain about which I feel a sense of mystery and awe.

Winnicott, too, seems to be aware of the impenetrability of the enigma of the space in which illusion is generated:

> [T]his matter of *illusion* [transitional objects and phenomena] is one that belongs inherently to human beings and that no individual finally solves for himself or herself, although a *theoretical* understanding of it may provide a *theoretical* solution.
>
> (p. 13)

Winnicott seems to be saying that he is not able to provide more than a theoretical understanding of transitional objects and phenomena, but that this shortcoming is inevitable and must be tolerated.

Winnicott describes the experience of letting go of the transitional object:

> Its fate is to be gradually allowed to be decathected, so that in the course of years it becomes not so much forgotten as relegated to limbo... It is not forgotten and it is not mourned. It loses meaning, and this is because transitional phenomena have become diffused, have become spread out over the whole... cultural field [the entire area of creative living].
>
> (p. 5)

While the original "Transitional object" paper was first delivered in 1951, it was not until 20 years later (in the version published in *Playing and Reality*) that Winnicott first uses the word *paradox* to describe transitional objects and phenomena, and when he does, he uses it only twice in a two-sentence paragraph at the end of the theoretical portion of the paper:

> What emerges from these considerations [of transitional objects and transitional phenomena] is the further idea that paradox accepted can have positive value. The resolution of the paradox leads to a defence organization which in the adult one can encounter in true and false self organization.
>
> (1971a, p. 14)

This passage is an important part of the paper, and yet it seems weakly stated as it describes the resolution of the paradox in terms of the creation of a particular defense organization. Winnicott makes a more articulate statement of the paradoxical nature of transitional objects and phenomena in the "Introduction" (1971d) to *Playing and Reality* (a book Winnicott opens with the "Transitional object" paper, and in succeeding chapters, develops many of its themes):

> I am drawing attention [in this book] to the *paradox* involved in the use by the infant of... the transitional object. My contribution is to ask for a paradox to be accepted and tolerated and respected, and for it not to be resolved. By flight to split-off intellectual functioning it is possible to resolve the paradox, but the price of this is the loss of the value of the paradox itself.
>
> (p. xii)

Paradox is not simply another metaphor Winnicott uses in his effort to understand the form of experiencing he is studying. It seems to me that with the idea of paradox he has arrived at a way of speaking about transitional objects and phenomena that not only serves as a way of *conceptualizing* these phenomena but also describes what it feels like to *experience* them. In both the experience of transitional phenomena and the concept of paradox, opposites coexist (without contradicting one another) in a way that creates something larger than the sum of the binary parts, something nonlinear that cannot be stated in any other way. Sustaining a paradox requires that we release our minds from secondary process thinking and allow the terms of the paradox to give way to something new, something with possibilities beyond those of logical thinking. *Paradox itself is born in the intermediate area of experiencing that it describes.*

Clinical material: Aspects of fantas

In the version of the "Transitional object" paper published in *Playing and Reality*, Winnicott adds a new section consisting of two clinical illustrations that reflect how his thinking "in regard to transitional phenomena affects what I see and hear and what I do" (p. 20). The first of these pieces of clinical work was twice previously published. The second was published for the first time in the 1971 version of the paper. The latter is the one I will be discussing in some detail because it illustrates with unusual clarity what I see as some of Winnicott's most highly evolved ways of being with and thinking about a patient, while leaving space for the reader to do something of his or her own with the clinical material.

Winnicott names the new clinical illustration "Aspects of Fantas" (p. 20). The word *fantas*, so far as I have been able to determine, is a neologism which immediately presents the reader with *an experience of the in between*—the space between invented language and language as ordinarily used. Fantas holds some similarity to fantasy, but they are not the same thing.

Winnicott introduces the session by saying that it is an example of "how the sense of loss itself can become a way of integrating one's self experience" (p. 20). This sentence is important to keep in mind as one becomes immersed in Winnicott's account of a single analytic session.

The patient is a highly intelligent woman, with several children, who comes to analysis with symptoms "usually collected together under the word 'schizoid'" (p. 21), a term which in 1971 refers to individuals who are preoccupied (and occupied) by their inner lives to a degree that leaves them largely cut off from real relationships with external objects; they also rely heavily on omnipotent thinking as a defense against the problems posed by life in their internal and external worlds. Nonetheless, Winnicott's patient is well liked and not suspected to be as ill as she is.

The session begins with a dream which is related to a "hankering after a former analyst" (p. 21). Winnicott does not tell us the dream, but says that the dream is "depressive" (a phenomenon of Klein's [1935] depressive position in which self-object differentiation has been achieved and the major anxieties are related to loss and depression) and "could be used as material for interpretation" (p. 21). But while it "could be used" for interpretation, Winnicott does not use the dream as material for interpretation. It is by means of omission of this sort that Winnicott quietly makes his point.

"Every now and again she is overtaken by what might be called *fantasying*" (p. 21), but here again Winnicott does not indicate that *he* would call it fantasying. Perhaps he would call it *fantas*. The patient imagines she is on a train journey in which there is an accident and her children and her analyst would not know what has happened to her. (Winnicott refers to himself impersonally as "her analyst.") "She might be screaming, but her mother would not hear" (p. 21). The patient then talks about "her most awful experience" (p. 21) when she left her cat to cry for several hours. This "joins up with the very many separations she experienced throughout her childhood" (p. 21), which went beyond what she could handle "and were therefore traumatic, necessitating the organization of new sets of defences" (p. 21).

Winnicott comments: "Much of the material of the analysis has to do with coming to the negative side of relationships; that is to say, with the gradual failure that has to be experienced by the child when the parents are not available" (p. 21). Here, Winnicott is reinventing the word *negative* by means of the way he is using it.[2] The term, in Winnicott's hands, refers both to the failure of the parents to be adequately available to the child and to the psychic failure (damage) suffered by the child as a consequence of the excessive absence of the parents.

The patient is upset by the failures of her mothering of her own children: she left her two-year-old child for three days when she went on holiday with her husband when she was pregnant with her second child. She was told that the child cried for four hours after she left, and it took a long time, on the patient's return, for the child to reestablish a connection with her.

> When no understanding can be given [to a child about a separation and a pregnancy], then when the mother is away to have a new baby she is dead from the point of view of the child. This is what dead means.
>
> (pp. 21–22)

Here, Winnicott is reinventing the word *dead*. *Dead* means the state of the mother, in the child's mind, whose physical and emotional absence is beyond the comprehension of her child and the duration of the absence is longer than the child can tolerate. This leads the child to defend himself or herself by means of emotional disconnection from the mother.

> It is a matter of days or hours or minutes. Before the limit is reached the mother is still alive; after this limit has been overstepped she is dead. In between is *a precious moment of anger*, but this is quickly lost, or perhaps never experienced, always potential and carrying fear of violence.
>
> (p. 22, italics added)

In response to the absence of the mother, there is a momentary opportunity to mitigate not only the pain of the loss but also the potential damage to the child ("the organization of new sets of defences") in response to the unmanageable loss. That momentary opportunity resides in "a precious moment of anger" that the child might experience. It seems to me that Winnicott is viewing this feeling of anger as a product of the child's capacity to actually perceive, feel, and understand what is happening in the world outside of himself or herself, and to respond to it with anger. It is a "precious moment of anger," I believe, because the child feels and expresses anger at the object who is present to receive it, accept it, live with it, and be changed by it. I would say it is not primarily the mother who dies when an unmanageable separation occurs, but it is the child who dies psychically. This, too, is what dead means.

The anger that is not experienced—when the child is forced to a point beyond what he or she can tolerate—remains a "potential" for the child, but the anger is denied expression because it carries a "fear of violence." To my mind, the object of the feared violence is not the mother, for she is dead, she no longer exists for the child; the child's anger is directed against himself or herself. This is what makes reclaiming that "precious moment of anger" in the analytic setting so difficult and so dangerous: the patient's life is at stake as a consequence of the anger directed against the self (the only person felt to be present).

> From here we come to the two extremes, so different from each other: the death of the mother when she is present, and her death when she is not able to reappear and therefore to come alive again.
>
> (p. 22)

The first of these extremes is the experience of the death of the mother who is emotionally present, and the child is able to experience and express his or her feelings in that precious moment of anger. The second is the death of the mother (and the child) when the child is unable to hold her psychically, as she is leaving, during her absence, and after her return. This mother is no longer alive to the child (and I would add, the child is no longer alive to himself or herself).

The patient, when she was about 11, was evacuated to live with a foster family during World War II.

> ... she completely forgot her childhood and her parents, but all the time she steadily maintained the right not to call those who were caring for her "uncle" and "auntie," which was the usual technique. She managed *never to call them anything* the whole of those years, and this was the negative of remembering her mother and father. It will be understood that the pattern for all this was set up in her early childhood.
>
> (p. 22)

The word *negative* appears here a second time and continues to be defined by the way Winnicott is using it. Earlier in the paper the word *negative* had to do with the psychic "failure" of the child, the damage done to the child by excessive unavailability of the parents. Now, a new layer of meaning is being added to the term. The patient's refusal to call her foster parents anything is the "negative of remembering," which is not synonymous with forgetting. The negative of remembering is a more active process than forgetting in that it involves a forceful rejection of the falsehood of the presence of "replacement parents," a rejection of the lie, a fierce hold on the truth; it is an affirmation of the realness of absence. The foster parents are not the patient's auntie and uncle, and so the patient refused to call them that.

Winnicott continues:

> From this my patient reached the position, which again comes into the transference, that the only real thing is the gap; that is to say, the death or the absence or the amnesia. In the course of the session she had a specific amnesia and this bothered her, and it turned out that the important communication for me to get was that there could be a blotting out, and that this blank could be the only fact and the only thing that was real. The amnesia is real, whereas what is forgotten has lost its reality.
>
> (p. 22)

All that feels real to the patient is the "blotting out," "the blank," and "the amnesia," but not the absent mother herself to whom she is amnesic. Nothing is forgotten because there is nothing real to forget. Longing is not the emotion the patient felt when she was evacuated during the war. Added to the idea of "the negative," here, is the idea that the experience of the negative involves both the feeling that nothing alive has been lost and the feeling that the nothing, itself, *is* what is alive and real. Let me put this in still another way. The opposite of present is not absent, for there is nothing absent that is real: the absent never was present and cannot return to presence from absence. Though Winnicott does not use the term "paradox," I would say that he is engaged in paradoxical thinking in his use of the concept of "the negative": *What is not recalled has not been forgotten. There is nothing to forget and nothing to remember because there has never been anything present that has felt real. The gap, the death, the nothing is what feels real.*

It is important to note that Winnicott, in this paper, rarely uses the terms "internal object relationships," "the ego," "the repression barrier," "the repressed, unconscious conflict," and the like; and in only a few instances, when speaking of the work of other analytic writers, does he use the term "unconscious." This is not to say that the topographic model is not an organizing schema in Winnicott's mind. Nonetheless, Winnicott is changing the language of psychoanalysis in both his theoretical and his clinical thinking. "The negative" refers to a quality of being alive in the realness of what is not there and supersedes the notion of the conscious and the unconscious mind. Is the experience of the amnesia, the gap, or the absence a conscious or an unconscious phenomenon? The question does not apply because the presence of the absence, the gap, the amnesia, or the negative pervades the entirety of the personality and does not lend itself to being categorized as conscious or unconscious. The qualities of aliveness and deadness, realness and unrealness transcend (know not the limits of) the qualities of consciousness and unconsciousness (Ogden, 2019, 2020). "For me the self, which is not the ego, is the person who is me, who is only me, who has a totality based on the operation of the maturational processes" (Winnicott, 1971e, quoted by Abram, 2013, p. 313).

Transference is no longer simply the act of experiencing the analyst as a projection of aspects of unconscious internal objects or object relationships (as it is for Freud, Klein, and Fairbairn). Transference, for Winnicott, also refers to the patient's experience of the analyst as real or unreal, alive or dead, truthful or untruthful, and "[i]t will be understood that the pattern for all this was set up in her early childhood" (p. 22).

Winnicott tells us that the patient once used a "rug" (a blanket) in his consulting room during an episode of regression, but she no longer uses it.

> The reason is that the rug that is not there (because she does not go for it) is more real than the rug the analyst might bring, as he certainly had the idea to do.
>
> (p. 22).

Winnicott again refers to himself not as "I" but as "the analyst" and refers to himself in the third person "he," even when talking about something he feels strongly about: "as he certainly had the idea to do." In this way he suggests that he is unreal to the patient (and perhaps to himself): he is, in the transference (and perhaps the countertransference), the negative of a real and present analyst.

The patient then tells Winnicott:

> The last of her former analysts "will always be more important to me than my present analyst." She added, "You may do me more good, but I like him better. This will be true when I have completely forgotten him. The negative of him is more real than the positive of you."
>
> (pp. 22–23)

There is now a hostile edge to the way the patient is talking to Winnicott. When the patient addresses Winnicott as "my present analyst," she seems to be treating him as she treated her foster parents by refusing to use the personal pronoun *you*. Despite the fact that he is physically present, he is not real to her. The patient introduces the idea of "the positive" when saying, "The negative of him is more real than the positive of you." The idea of "the positive," here, has taken on an unexpected meaning: present, but unreal.

The paradox with which the patient and Winnicott are dealing at this moment of the session might now be put in a more distilled form: *absence is presence* and *presence is absence*. It is tempting to try to resolve this paradox (understand it in a linear way), but it is only in the form of the unresolved paradox that the truth of the phenomenon can be sensed.

The case discussion becomes a bit fragmented at this point as Winnicott describes the patient's imaginings as a child—an angel at the foot of her bed, an eagle chained to her wrist, and a toy white horse with whom she "would ride... everywhere together" (p. 23). The patient then says, "I suppose I want something that never goes away" (p. 23). "We formulated this by saying that the real thing is the thing that is not here" (p. 23). Note that Winnicott does not say that he "interpreted" or "showed the patient"; he says, "We formulated."

The patient describes methods she used for dealing with separation: "a paper spider and pulling the legs off for every day that her mother was away" (p. 24), a technique that seems to me to reflect the patient's dismembering of herself, becoming less whole and less real to herself each day of her mother's absence. She goes on to experience "a flash" (p. 24) in which she sees her toy dog named Toby—"Oh there's Toby" (p. 24)—whom she remembers only in these flashes.

> This led on to a terrible incident in which her mother had said to her: "But we 'heard' you cry all the time we were away." They were four miles apart. She was two years old at the time and she thought: "Could it possibly be that my mother told me a lie?" She was not able to cope with this at the time and she tried to deny what she really knew to be true, that her mother had in fact lied. It was difficult to believe in her mother in this guise because everyone said: "Your mother is so marvelous."
>
> (p. 24)

Curiously, Winnicott makes no mention of the strong resemblance between the patient's "remembered" experience of her mother (when the patient was two years old) and the patient's experience with her own child when he was two years old: he "had cried for four hours without stopping" (p. 21) when she left him for three days. The patient repeated with her own child what had occurred in her childhood. Winnicott appears to be taking at face value the patient's memory of something that occurred when she was two, but I do not think that that is what he is doing. He is not concerned with the question of whether the patient's "story" is a memory or a fantasy or a "fantas." He seems to me to take what the patient says as a communication, not as a statement of fact or of fantasy, perhaps something born in the intermediate space between fantasy and reality.

Winnicott says that he and the patient "reached to an idea that was rather new from my point of view" (p. 24):

> Here was the picture of a child and the child had transitional objects [Toby, the toy dog, and the toy white horse]... and all of these were symbolical of something and were real for the child; but gradually, or perhaps frequently for a little while, she had to *doubt the reality of the thing that they were symbolizing*. That is to say, if they were symbolical of her mother's devotion and reliability they remained real in themselves but what they stood for was not real. The mother's devotion and reliability were unreal.
>
> (p. 24)

Transitional objects depend on the reality of a loving, reliable relationship with the actual mother, and when that love and reliability are no longer present, the transitional object cannot be maintained, and it becomes an ordinary object, a *thing* that lacks the power to be soothing and comforting and alive. As a result of the fact that her mother's love had become unreal, all that the patient possessed were toys that were mere *things*, no longer transitional objects. This, too, is what dead means.

The patient then said, "All I have got is what I have not got" (p. 24).

Winnicott, at this point, writes what is for me one of the most important sentences in this clinical account:

> There is a desperate attempt here to turn the negative into a last-ditch defence against the end of everything. The negative is the only positive.
>
> (p. 24)

The patient is using the negative—an emptiness, a gap in her own being—which feels real, as a last-ditch form of protection against her own psychic death, "the end of everything."

In saying, "The negative is the only positive," and the "positive" no longer refers simply to what is present, but unreal; it seems to refer now to an absence (a gap) that feels real, but is on the edge of feeling inadequate to preserve the patient's sanity, her self.

> When she got to this point [after saying, "All I have got is what I have not got"] she said to her analyst: "And what will you do about it?" I was silent and she said: "Oh, I see." I thought perhaps she was resenting my masterly inactivity. I said: "I am silent because I don't know what to say." She quickly said that this was all right. Really she was glad about the silence, and she would have preferred it if I had said nothing at all.
>
> (p. 24)

For me, the session breaks open here. There is something quite new in the patient's tone of voice as she asks, "And what will you do about it?" Here, the patient acknowledges Winnicott's presence and places him squarely in the room with her by using the personal pronoun *you* in her question/demand. Winnicott seems startled and at a bit of a loss to know what is happening. He tells us, "I was silent and she said: 'Oh, I see.'" Winnicott says he imagines that the patient is derisively viewing him as "masterly" in the role of the stereotypic passive analyst.

Winnicott responds, "I am silent because I don't know what to say," a response I (and perhaps the patient) find disarmingly honest. "She quickly said that this was all right. Really she was glad about the silence, and she would have preferred it if I had said nothing at all." I startle each time I read these two sentences. The patient is talking to Winnicott in a way that conveys that she knows precisely what she wants and needs (silence), and what she does not want and does not need (Winnicott's words of apology). She is quietly assertive, a bit angry and impatient, but also, as I imagine her at this moment, subtly playful.

As I read this passage, there seem to be two things happening at once. It is an opportunity for the patient to feel and express that precious moment of anger. And at the same time, it seems to me that the patient is telling Winnicott that she would prefer he be silent because she wants and needs to be alone with herself, alone with the experience of what Winnicott (1963) describes as her *"permanently non-communicating"* (Winnicott, 1963, p. 187) core self, which "is sacred and most worthy of preservation" (p. 187).

The latter possibility is supported by the sentence that immediately follows (in the same paragraph): "Perhaps as a silent analyst I might have been joined up with the former analyst that she knows she will always be looking for" (p. 24), an analyst whom the patient is fond of and will become "sunk in the [patient's] general pool of subjectivity" (p. 25). Perhaps, at this moment in the session, Winnicott feels that something is changing: his presence, joined up with that of the previous analyst may, without representational definition, be in the process of becoming integrated into the patient's very being, her "general pool of subjectivity."

He continues to muse about what "her meaning was" (p. 25). Perhaps he and the previous analyst would also be "joined up with what she thought she found when she had a mother and before she began to notice her mother's deficiencies as a mother, that is to say, her absences" (p. 25). The meaning of this sentence is difficult for me to understand, so I must write Winnicott here in addition to reading him. Perhaps the patient will retain in her central core a version of her mother she thought she had—a reliable, devoted mother—before she lost her mother when "she began to notice her mother's deficiencies." Even though she was to later lose her mother, she once "thought... she had a mother" who was genuinely a mother to her. This benign version of her mother, a real mother, is coming to the fore as the patient tells Winnicott she would prefer he be silent (perhaps to allow her to be alone with herself in his presence [Winnicott, 1958b]).

The session continues to change as it draws toward a close with "a bit of a game" (p. 25). The patient tells Winnicott a story in which he is accompanying her on a train journey she is actually about to take to visit her holiday house.

> [S]he said: "Well I think you had better come with me, perhaps half-way." She was talking about the way in which it matters to her very much indeed that she is leaving me.
>
> (p. 25)

In the patient's story, "after a little while, when she has got away from me, it will not matter any longer" (p. 25). It seems to me that in the story the patient is telling Winnicott, she hopes there is a half-way point where she will forget Winnicott. It is not yet clear whether at the half-way point she removes him from her mind (leaving a gap) or keeps him with her in her mind.

> So, at a half-way station, I [Winnicott] get out and "come back in the hot train", and she derided my maternal identification aspects by adding: "And it will be very tiring, and there will be a lot of children and babies, and they will climb all over you, and they will probably be sick all over you, and serve you right."
>
> (p. 25)

At a half-way station, Winnicott will "come back"—not "go back"—so the patient, in this sense, is with Winnicott on his return home. He is alive to her in the story; she is with him, even as she is leaving him. The tender, childlike tone of the patient's voice as she tells him her story is quite different from the complex sound of her voice asking, "And what will you do about it?" Winnicott has remained alive and present for the patient, and she has been able to experience with him that "precious moment of anger" in her earlier question/demand, and now offers a much more playful expression of her anger in response to his anticipated absence. She tells him that on his return trip by himself "there will be a lot of children and babies… and they will probably be sick all over you, and serve you right." This is what alive means.

The session concludes:

> Just before she went she said, "Do you know I believe when I went away at the time of evacuation [in the war] I could say that *I went to see if my parents were there*. I seem to have believed I would find them there." (This implied that they were certainly not to be found at home.) And the implication was that she took a year or two to find the answer. The answer was that they were not there, and *that* was reality.
>
> (p. 25)

This part of the session involves a return to the patient's feeling: "All I have got is what I have not got." Here, at the end of the session, she makes an additional discovery—when she was evacuated during the war, she was looking to see if she would find her parents where she was sent, and Winnicott infers from this that they were clearly not to be found at home, and that absence, that gap, was what was real to her. This recognition that she was looking for her parents (and not finding them anywhere) during the evacuation seems to me to be both a genuine discovery and a gift to Winnicott for what the patient has experienced with him during the session: her discovery that "*no rug* can… be more important than *a* rug" (p. 25); her having the opportunity to express her anger at him in her demand "And what will you do about it?"; and her experience of playing with Winnicott as she told him her story of their separation during the train journey. (Though Winnicott does not mention it, the train journey at the end of the session is a transformed version of the train journey the patient was "*fantasying*" [p. 21] at the beginning of the session in which there was an accident, and the patient was screaming and not able to contact "her analyst" or her mother or anyone else.)

The mind swirls as negative and positive, real and unreal, alive and dead, internal and external, creating and discovering, truth and falsehood, transform themselves into one another like the sides of a Mobius strip, but this must be tolerated because it is the way the mind grows and the way analysis works in the intermediate area of experiencing.

Clinical illustration: An invisible man

Mr. Y began analysis shortly after he wrote a suicide note to the director of a training program in which he was enrolled. He was put on indefinite medical leave by the director. The patient explained to me that he had not felt suicidal when he wrote the note. He wanted to leave the training program, but did not know how to go about doing it. In our first session, Mr. Y told me that he had been an avid reader from the time he was very young. He loved the feel of the heft of books in his hands, he loved reading, but he could remember hardly anything of what he read. I said to him that his description of reading made me think of a baby who sucks at the breast vigorously, but the milk drips from his mouth, and if this is not noticed and responded to, the baby may starve to death.

During the initial years of this long five-session-per-week analysis, Mr. Y told me that his mother had married when she was a 19-year-old college student, and his father, a successful attorney, was a decade older than she. A few days before they married, his father drove his own parents halfway across the country without stopping, except for meals. His father fell asleep at the wheel and the car crashed, killing the patient's grandfather. The wedding went on as planned. Mr. Y's mother became pregnant with the patient shortly before the wedding. The patient's father insisted she drop out of college to care for the patient, which she did, but deeply resented the patient for it. Mr. Y spoke with little feeling in his voice as he told me about these events.

The patient's parents stayed together, he said, despite the fact that they had virtually nothing to do with one another. They had their own bedrooms and his father never took his meals with the patient, his mother, and his younger sister. His mother rarely left the house—she ordered groceries by telephone and bought clothes from catalogs. It seemed to Mr. Y that his mother waited all day for his sister to get home from school, and when she arrived home, his mother was eager to hear every detail of what had happened during her day at school. His mother seemed to the patient to have no interest in being his mother. From the time he was three or four years old, he came and went from the house unnoticed and wandered the streets, which sometimes led him to feel invisible and at other times, terrified.

After giving me an initial detailed account of his life, he said he did not know what to talk about. The sessions became marked by long silences between the patient's brief, rather empty, accounts of events at work or in the lives of his wife and two children.

Mr. Y never missed a session and was almost never late. We talked about the way the silence in the sessions felt to him like his mother's silence when he was with her. But in our discussions of these and related events, I felt the patient was talking *about himself* without actually being present *as himself*. My reveries felt like dreams that were not dreams (Bion, 1960; Ogden, 2003), that is, dreams that accomplish no psychological work. Mr. Y occasionally told me about the pleasure he took in playing board games with his children and watching television with them, but at these times it seemed to me that he was trying to win my approval.

Over the years, the patient filled the sessions in a range of ways, including long silences, hammering me with questions (more than 50 each session), arguing points of view he did not believe in, talking at great length about topics that he did not care about, detailed accounts of situations in which the story was told from the point of view of someone other than the patient, and the like. He seemed to ignore what I said to him during these (superficially) different sorts of sessions.

This state of affairs continued for more than ten years, during which time I could see little change in the patient. I came to dread the sessions, which felt interminable. I considered ending the analysis and referring Mr. Y to someone who might be able to work with him, since I felt I could not.

I began a session in the 11th year of the analysis by saying to Mr. Y that it seemed to me that the analysis was not resulting in change in him either during the sessions or in his life outside the analysis. I said that some sessions began with a promise of something that might occur that felt real, but as time went on that proved not to be happening. I proposed that when it seemed to either of us that we had done what we could do in a session, one or the other of us would say so, and at that point I would read in my chair behind the couch and he could read something he brought to the session or simply remain quiet. We would resume talking when either of us felt we had something we wanted to say that we actually believed.

The patient said, "I wouldn't want to lie here while you're having an interesting conversation with whoever wrote the book you're reading. I'd rather leave."

It seemed to me that, for Mr. Y, my reading would feel like a replication of his experience of listening to his mother and sister talking, but I did not say this to him. Instead, I said, "All right, why don't we end the session when either of us feels that we've done what we can for that day." (I had not proposed a radical alteration of the frame of this sort, or even considered doing so, with any other patient I had worked with, nor have I done so since.) I worried that this alteration of the frame would feel punitive to Mr. Y, but this possibility seemed preferable to ending the analysis altogether, which was the only alternative I could imagine at that point.

During the first few sessions following the introduction of this change, Mr. Y spoke more than he had in recent sessions, but as was often the case, it did not seem to me that he cared about what he was saying. I chose not to end these sessions early. After several more sessions, the patient took charge and ended, about 15 minutes early, a session that was almost entirely silent. The following day Mr. Y came in and said:

> While I was walking from your office to my car yesterday after I ended the session early, I had an idea that I wanted to tell you right away, but since I couldn't, I wrote it down as soon as I got to my car. Would it be all right if I read it to you?

I said that it would. Mr. Y then read me what he had written, but after he finished, he said that it sounded flat as he read it, even though when he was thinking it and writing it down, it felt very interesting, but it had all evaporated. "It's gone now," he said.

I replied, "What you were thinking and what you wrote down aren't here now, but the feeling you had as you were thinking and writing them isn't gone. That feeling was real and it left you with something real." It was significant that his experience had occurred "during our 50-minute session" even though the patient was outside of the consulting room for that part of the session.

I would remain in my chair behind the couch for the remainder of the session after Mr. Y left early and would sometimes write down what I was thinking and feeling. Some time into this period of work, I had a reverie after the session was ended early. A gang of the most terrifying men was chasing me. There was no doubt in my mind that they would torture me before killing me. Instead of trying to find a way to kill them or escape from them, which seemed impossible, I tried to find a way of killing myself before they caught me and tortured me. But I couldn't find a way of doing it. My heart was pounding when I "awoke" from this reverie. During the remainder of the session, I thought about the patient's method of dealing with the pain of growing up absolutely alone, with neither a mother nor a father. I was reminded of his suicide note that he had not realized was an actual suicide note, of his reading in a way that left him utterly empty, and of his isolation from his mother, his father, his wife, his children, and me—while not being able to find a way of completely doing away with himself.

The patient began the next session by saying:

> When I was walking to my car after our session yesterday, after you ended it early, I was talking to you in my head, telling you that you had tricked me into this new thing we're doing, and you've tricked other patients in the same way. But that feeling is gone, too.

After a period of silence, Mr. Y said, "Every word I say here sounds like an echo, not my actual voice. I get bored listening to my voice; in fact, I can't stand it, it's not... I don't know... it's just not."

I said, "*It's* just not, and *you're* just not."

"The best part of the session is after I leave here, but that dissolves when I get back here." After pausing, he added, "I only have myself to talk to... but I didn't used to have even that."

I said:

> I think that from the time you were a small child you've been so lonely and so empty that you've been looking for a way to kill yourself, but you haven't been able to find one because you want to remain alive when you die.

(It was only as I said this to Mr. Y that I realized that the particular alteration of the frame I had devised lent itself to the experience of remaining alive after the end, after death.)

The patient responded, "I shouldn't tell you this but I like leaving the session early, particularly when it's dark outside. I like it because I have time to myself in the dark—I can think then." (This is what alive means, for Mr. Y, at this moment.)

The "agreement" to end the session when one of us felt we had done what we could do for that day continued for six or seven months. When one of us ended the session early, I felt we were doing something other than passively allowing the silence or meaningless talk to drown us (kill us) as Mr. Y had died in childhood. It seemed to me the patient, from the earliest years of his life, was surviving, not growing—which had also been the case in the analysis for so many years. I began to realize during the period of the alteration of the frame that Mr. Y's talk rang empty or untrue to me because he was not a sufficiently whole person, a sufficiently living individual, to know what felt real or unreal to him. The experience of the patient's death in childhood took the form of unrelenting empty silence and meaningless talk in the sessions, which was difficult for both the patient and me to bear. That experience became less suffocating (less lethal) as the patient began to be able to experience his feelings and to think, at first outside the consulting room during the sessions and later inside the consulting room.

Gradually, each of us let go of the practice of ending a session early, but the experience we had had during that period—the experience of the patient's beginning to come to life during the part of the session in which he was outside of the consulting room, outside of the experience of his own death—continued to play a central role in the analysis in the years that followed.

As I write about the alteration of the frame in my work with Mr. Y, I am reminded of Winnicott's idea that his patient's fierce attachment to the negative, to the realness of the gap, was "a last-ditch defence against the end of everything" (p. 24). In my work with Mr. Y, my alteration of the frame felt like a last-ditch effort against the end of the analysis, against the patient and I drowning in the patient's death in childhood, and against the end of everything.

I will close by briefly discussing some of the work of Bion, Symington, Pick, and Coltart which contributed to the state of mind in which I "decided" to introduce the radical alteration of the analytic frame in my work with Mr. Y. Among those influences was an exchange that occurred in one of Bion's (1978) clinical discussions. A presenter says that his patient "is afraid that if she got a divorce from her husband she would run around and have sex with all sorts of men—behave like a free whore" (p. 259). The presenter further explains that the patient feels like a whore because her father has implied this, and she is afraid that he, the analyst, will come to the same conclusion. Bion responds:

> In view of what you are saying I think I would try to draw her attention to the way in which she wishes to limit my freedom about what I call her... Why shouldn't I be free to form my own opinion that she's a whore or that she is something quite different?
>
> (p. 259)

Bion, here, is underscoring the importance of the analyst's freedom to think, to have any thought he will, despite the patient's conscious or unconscious efforts to prevent him from doing so. In my work with Mr. Y, for many years preceding my altering the frame, it was very difficult for me to manage psychic survival, much less freedom of thought.

Symington takes up where Bion leaves off concerning the analyst's freedom to think. For Symington, such freedom depends upon the analyst's capacity to release himself from "a certain [restrictive] patterning of unconscious knowledge" (p. 290). From the outset, the analytic pair becomes part of a single "corporate entity" (p. 290) from which the analyst must recover his identity as an analyst capable of, and responsible for, independent thought. In my work with Mr. Y, the restrictive "unconscious patterning" took the form of an unconsciously shared set of assumptions regarding the limits of our capacity for aliveness combined with the fear of aliveness. This complex set of feelings was depicted in my reverie in which my life was threatened, I was trying to find a way to kill myself, and I was not able to find a way of doing so.

Pick (1985) focuses on the way the patient's projections are "'mated' with [unconscious] parts of the analyst" (p. 161) which are difficult for the analyst to emotionally process, yet central to the patient's psychic problems. She notes that patients are quite adept at projecting aspects of themselves into specific aspects of the analyst. "The patient is consciously or unconsciously mindful as to whether the analyst evades or meets the issues [which are at the core of the patient's psychic problems]" (p. 165). In my work with Mr. Y, the conscious and unconscious experiences of deadness brought me close to ending the analysis (which would have served to evade confronting the issue of psychic aliveness and deadness, for my own sake as well as the patient's).

Coltart (1985) discusses the importance of our being willing "to be continually open to the emergence of the unexpected" (p. 6). She says, "in analysis it is true to say that one does not *think* at all during some sessions, at least in the ordinary cognitive use of the word" (p. 8). And when we have helped the patient effect psychic growth, "It would be unwise to conclude that... we actually *know* how it was *done*" (p. 14). Coltart here provides me with words to describe my uncertainty concerning the way the idea of altering the frame "came to me." Moreover, I cannot say I understand how this alteration led the patient to make good analytic use of the part of the session that occurred when he was outside of my consulting room. The "shape" of the analysis at that juncture seemed to emerge of its own accord once the pieces, internal and external, were more or less in place.

Notes

1 While it is beyond the scope of this paper to review the many publications on Winnicott's "Transitional objects and transitional phenomena," the following have been significant influences on the development of my thinking: Abram, 2007; Civitarese, 2016; Copolillo, 1976; Elmhirst, 1980; Ferro & Molinari, 2016; Gabbard, 1994; Gaddini, 2003; Gaddini & Gaddini, 1970; Green, 1997, 1999; Greenacre, 1970; Grolnick et al., 1978; McKay, 2019; Quatman, 2020; Rudnytsky, 1993; Williams, 2007.

2 Andre Green (1997), having treated this same patient after Winnicott's death, develops his own idea of the negative which he believes corrects, among other things, "the important censorship in sexuality in Winnicott's paper" (p. 1079).

References

Abram, J. (2007). *The Language of Winnicott: A Dictionary of Winnicott's Use of Words,* 2nd edition. London: Routledge.

Abram, J. (2013). DWW's notes for the Vienna Congress 1971. A consideration of Winnicott's theory of aggression and an interpretation of the clinical implications. In *Donald Winnicott Today,* ed. J. Abram. London: Routledge, pp. 302–330.

Bion, W. R. (1978). Four discussions. In *Clinical Seminars and Other Works,* ed. F. Bion. London: Karnac, pp. 241–292.

Bion, W. R. (1960). *Learning from Experience.* London: Tavistock.

Civitarese, G. (2016). On sublimation. *Int. J. Psychoanal.* 97: 1369–1392.

Coltart, N. (1985). Slouching towards Bethlehem. In *Slouching Towards Bethlehem.* New York: Guilford, 1992, pp. 1–14.

Copolillo, H. P. (1976). The transitional phenomenon revisited. *J. Am. Acad. Child Psychiatry* 15: 36–47.

Elmhirst, S. I. (1980). Transitional objects in transition. *Int. J. Psychoanal.* 61: 367–373.

Ferro, A., & Molinari, E. (2016). Discussion of "Peter the child who could not dream." *Psychoanal. Inq.* 36: 239–241.

Gabbard, G. O. (1994). Sexual excitement and countertransference love in the analyst. *J. Amer. Psychoanal. Assn.* 42: 1083–1106.

Gaddini, R. (2003). The precursors of transitional objects and phenomena. *Psychoanal. Hist.* 5: 53–61.

Gaddini, R., & Gaddini, E. (1970). Transitional objects and the process of individuation: A study of three different social groups. *J. Amer. Acad. Child Psychiatry* 9: 347–365.

Green, A. (1997). The intuition of the negative in *Playing and Reality. Int. J. Psychoanal.* 78: 1071–1084.

Green, A. (1999). *The Work of the Negative.* London: Free Association Press.

Greenacre, P. (1970). The transitional object and the fetish with special reference to the role of illusion. *Int. J. Psychoanal.* 51: 447–455.

Grolnick, S., Barkin, L., & Muensterberger, W. (eds.) (1978). *Between Fantasy and Reality: Transitional Objects and Phenomena.* New York: Aronson.

Klein, M. (1935). A contribution to the psychogenesis of manic-depressive states. *Int. J. Psychoanal.* 16: 145–174.

McKay, R. (2019). Where objects were, subjects now may be. The work of Jessica Benjamin and reimagining maternal subjectivity in transitional space. *Psychoanal. Inq.* 39: 163–173.

Ogden, T. H. (1995). Analysing forms of aliveness and deadness of the transference-countertransference. *Int. J. Psychoanal.* 76: 695–710.

Ogden, T. H. (2003). On not being able to dream. *Int. J. Psychoanal.* 84: 17–30.

Ogden, T. H. (2019). Ontological psychoanalysis or "What do you want to be when you grow up?" *Psychoanal. Q.* 88: 661–684.

Ogden, T. H. (2020). Toward a revised form of analytic thinking and practice: The evolution of analytic theory of mind. *Psychoanal. Q.* 89: 219–243.

Pick, I. B. (1985). Working through in the countertransference. *Int. J. Psychoanal.* 66: 157–166.

Quatman, T. (2020). *Accessing the Clinical Genius of Winnicott: A Careful Reading of Winnicott's Twelve Most Essential Papers*. London: Routledge.

Rudnytsky, P. (1993). *Transitional Objects and Potential Spaces: Literary Uses of D. W. Winnicott*. New York: Columbia University Press.

Symington, N. (1983). The analyst's act of freedom as agent of therapeutic change. *Int. R. Psychoanal.* 10: 283–291.

Williams, P. (2007). The worm that flies in the night. *Brit. J. Psychother.* 23: 343–364.

Winnicott, D. W. (1953). Transitional objects and transitional phenomena: A study of the first not-me possession. *Int. J. Psychoanal.* 34: 89–97.

Winnicott, D. W. (1958a). Transitional objects and transitional phenomena: A study of the first not-me possession. In *Through Paediatrics to Psycho-Analysis*. New York: Basic Books, 1975, pp. 229–242.

Winnicott, D. W. (1958b). The capacity to be alone. In *The Maturational Processes and the Facilitating Environment*. New York:International Universities Press, 1965, pp. 29–36.

Winnicott, D. W. (1969). The use of an object and relating through identifications. In *Playing and Reality*. New York: Basic Books, 1971, pp. 86–94.

Winnicott, D. W. (1971a). Transitional objects and transitional phenomena. In *Playing and Reality*. London: Routledge, pp. 1–25.

Winnicott, D. W. (1971b). *Playing and Reality*. London: Routledge.

Winnicott, D. W. (1971c). The place where we live. In *Playing and Reality*. London: Routledge, pp. 104–110.

Winnicott, D. W. (1971d). Introduction. In *Playing and Reality*. London: Routledge, pp xi–xiii.

Winnicott, D. W. (1971e). Le corps et le self, V. N. Smirnoff, trans. [Body and self]. *Nouv. Rev. Psychanal.* 3: 15–51.

3 Rethinking the concept of the unconscious

In recent years, my attention has been drawn to fundamental ideas underlying the way I think analytically. In doing so, I have come to rethink the concepts of the unconscious mind and time in the analytic setting. I offer a set of speculative thoughts as a personal approach to reconsidering these two psychoanalytic concepts. This paper is meant not to convince but to invite imaginative response.

The concept of the unconscious

It may seem heretical for a psychoanalyst to say that there is no such entity as the unconscious. After all, Freud, and almost all psychoanalysts, past and present, would argue that Freud's concept of the unconscious is definitive of psychoanalysis. I concur with this sentiment. Nonetheless, I submit that there is no such entity as the unconscious. This, at first, may be difficult to accept, particularly for psychoanalysts who have made use of the idea in every corner of our thinking for most of our lives. The reader may ask, "How could the unconscious be just an idea if it has afforded so much clarity of thinking?" The reader might also object to the idea that there is no such thing as the unconscious by saying that the unconscious may not be a thing, but it certainly is an experience. I would ask, "What experience are you referring to?" and the reader might say that dreaming is such an experience. I would counter: the dreams one remembers are conscious phenomena and those one cannot remember are forgotten thoughts like other thoughts or experiences that one cannot remember.

Freud (1915) claims that the existence of the unconscious is "incontrovertible" because of the meanings rendered available to conscious awareness when one makes use of the concept:

> A gain in meaning is a perfectly justifiable ground for going beyond the limits of direct experience [to justify acceptance of the existence of the unconscious mind]. When, in addition, it turns out that the assumption of there being an unconscious enables us to construct a successful procedure by which we can exert an effective influence upon the course

DOI: 10.4324/9781003528821-4

of conscious processes [for example, psychoanalytic treatment], this success will have given us an incontrovertible proof of the existence of what we have assumed.

(p. 167)

In other words, the claim that the unconscious exists is based on the success that the assumption has had in helping us understand the meanings of our experience that lie beyond conscious awareness. I am suggesting that the unconscious is an idea, a brilliant idea, but it is not an entity, even though the idea helps us make inferences about the meanings of our experience, as we do when making inferences in the analytic setting.

The unconscious, for Freud (1900, 1915), is a realm, a domain existing outside of conscious awareness in which unacceptable, impulsive, forbidden, threatening, shameful, guilt-ridden thoughts, feelings, and phantasies "reside." But despite Freud's insistence on this model of the mind, we must recognize that this domain or realm is a metaphor in which the conscious and unconscious aspects of mind exist. But this metaphor is not a mapping of the mind, for there is no "there" to map. Nothing can occur *there*, for there is no *there*. I have spent much of my life thinking of the unconscious as if it existed "below" the conscious mind, a "deeper" place in which primary process thinking and a quality of timelessness predominate. I have pictured the unconscious mind as a cellar in which repressed thoughts and feelings are buried and bang on the door (manned by censorship) for admittance or readmittance to the conscious domain of "clock time" and secondary process thinking.

I have found, and still find, the concept of the unconscious to be indispensable in my thinking about what is occurring in an analytic session and in my everyday life. I could not do my work as an analyst without it. But now I must remind myself that the unconscious exists only in the story created by Freud and subsequent psychoanalytic thinkers. There is no "inner world" (inside what?); nor are there object relationships inside of it; nor are there alpha-elements, beta-elements, alpha-function; there is no id, ego, or superego; no life instinct and death instinct, and so on. All of these are characters, forces, and organizers in stories written by psychoanalysts.

The name we give the unconscious is telling: it is "un" (without) conscious awareness, but we do not know the nature of this "un." We never have direct knowledge of it. We believe we "know about it" by inference as we create narratives concerning the meanings we read into "it." But the meanings we create are not evidence that there is an unconscious domain. What is a domain of the mind?

A dream is an experience played out in visual imagery that the individual remembers on waking. It must be kept in mind that when we wake up, we are no longer dealing with the dream experience we had while dreaming the dream. What we experience while dreaming is a conscious, not an unconscious, phenomenon, otherwise we would not be aware of it. When we wake up, we may remember something of a dream experience, but on waking we are elaborating the experience by placing it in the context of conscious, secondary process thinking and sequential time. It is not the unconscious that we remember on waking from a dream, but it is a conscious experience (otherwise we could not remember it) that occurred while sleeping that we remember on waking.

I submit that the unconscious is not a place or a thing, but it is a quality of one's thinking, feeling, and experiencing. The phenomena that we call the unconscious are experiences, qualities of consciousness[1]—which is not to be confused with Freud's conscious mind—that hold latent meaning. Freud's conception of the unconscious is invaluable for the way he understands the qualities of the thinking he attributes to the unconscious mind. Nevertheless, the latent meanings of dreams and other aspects of consciousness at which we arrive are not evidence of the existence of the unconscious; they are evidence of the success we have in understanding latent meanings of consciousness. Consciousness—the totality of our experiencing selves—is all we have available to us when we attempt to understand the latent meanings of experience.

One might object to the assertion that the unconscious mind is only an idea by asking, "Don't dreams reflect the individual's hidden wishes and fears?" "Hasn't it been shown by Freud and innumerable other analysts that dreams reflect the dreamer's wishes and fears that he or she dares not think or feel?" "Isn't a dream the individual's coming to life in ways he or she has not dared to do in waking life?" "Don't dreams help us locate ourselves and help us get a sense of what's going on with us emotionally?" I would answer "yes" to all of these questions. But none of these ideas serves as evidence that the unconscious mind is more than a concept.

Dreams are forms of thinking, but that does not make them evidence that there is such a thing as the unconscious mind; rather dream-thinking is evidence that we experience ourselves differently and think differently when asleep and can learn about ourselves by looking into the latent meaning of this experience. Freud introduced valuable ways of discerning latent meanings of the visual presentations experienced while dreaming. But latent meaning is just that, latent meaning, not evidence that the unconscious is anything more than an idea.

What is involved in coming to understand latent meaning of dreams might be more clearly understood by comparing that work with that of understanding latent meanings in literature. In reading a literary text, whether it be fiction or nonfiction, poetry or a theater script, meaning is not found *behind* the words or *under* the words; meaning resides *in* the words and the effects they create. We listen *to* the words, not *through* them. When we engage with a text, we are doing something with it, we are experiencing it, and at times we are putting into words our understanding of meanings latent in the words, but there is nothing there behind the words.

Conceiving of the unconscious as a phenomenon that occurs somewhere is to make an error similar to the one that we make when we conceive of the mind as a thing occupying a place inside our head or next to our head or somewhere else (Winnicott, 1949). Unlike the brain, the mind is not a noun, it is a verb, a phenomenon always in the process of change. William James (1890) conceives of the mind as a "stream of consciousness"; the mind is the act of experiencing, thinking, feeling, and narrating. We may be able to describe the way we think the mind works, but in doing so, we are making the error of positing an entity that exists somewhere and is the originator ("the prime mover," the ultimate origin) of the phenomena we experience (thoughts, feelings, sensations, dreams, and so on).

All we have available to us is consciousness, which is to be distinguished from Freud's conscious mind. As I mentioned earlier, what I mean by consciousness is the capacity to experience our thoughts, feelings, and sensations, and with development, the capacity to engage in a form of self-reflection in which we observe ourselves and talk to ourselves from a perspective in which we are both subject and object, I and me. Nothing lies "below" or "behind" consciousness. We may find that dividing consciousness into two strands— conscious and unconscious—helps us think about our analytic work, but consciousness does not come in strands; it is what it is in its indissoluble experiential unity.

I find a comment by Paul Eluard (1968) valuable in reconceiving Freud's conception of the "unconscious": "There is another world, but it is in this one." Freud's unconscious is another world, but it is in this one, in consciousness, not behind it or below it. What Freud called the unconscious is a quality of consciousness, not a realm that exists behind the repression barrier.

So how do I propose we think of our experience if the unconscious is just an idea? I would suggest that we say that we make inferences concerning consciousness which is the totality of what we know and experience. If we think of what we are doing as making inferences about consciousness, we avoid the error of positing the existence of another mind, another world, which does not exist. We know that consciousness exists and that it holds latent meanings. To say this is not to suggest that we not use the concept of the unconscious, but it is to say that when we use the idea, we should be aware that it is just an idea, not a place, not a second mind.

Clinical illustration

When I met Ms. V in the waiting room for our first meeting, she stood abruptly when she saw the door open and looked into my eyes pleadingly, as if looking for instruction concerning how she should behave. She appeared to be in her early 20s, dressed in a plain blouse and pleated skirt that were strikingly unfashionable. I introduced myself. She nodded and followed me into the consulting room where she waited for me to indicate where she should sit. Once seated, she continued to look at me for instructions. When I was silent, she said she had been asked to leave her doctoral program and then paused, waiting for me to respond.

I said, "It's natural not to know what you're supposed to do here."

She sighed and said, "I don't know what I'm supposed to do anywhere."

Ms. V told me that she was asked to leave her doctoral program for "failure to follow instructions." She said she has been working in a high-end women's clothing store where she's been having problems because she always seems to be saying the wrong thing.

I said, "There is a disconnect between what you intend to say and how it is taken."

"Yes, I'm always saying the wrong thing. I end up insulting customers when I'm only trying to help them find something they like. That's what happens but I don't want it to. My mother hates me. I'm not like her. I'm not feminine enough or pretty enough for her. I should be skinnier. She hates fat people. She likes my younger sister. My father loves me. He lets me go on rounds with him at the hospital. I'm too old for that, I know, but I did it as a kid and I've never wanted to give it up".

Ms. V stopped herself and said, "Aren't you supposed to ask me questions?"

"To tell you the truth, I don't know what I'm supposed to do."

"You don't have to ..."

"No, there isn't anything I have to do."

She said, "Is there anything wrong with going on hospital rounds with my father?"

"You're not sure."

"My mother says it's not right, but she hates everything about me. I like to go on rounds with him. When I was younger, we pretended I was a nurse assisting him."

"You felt you were someone when you were being your father's nurse."

Ms. V looked around my consulting room. "You've got a lot of books. Have you read all of them?"

"Some of them."

"You're old."

"I am." This observation felt more alive to me than anything she had said to this point. She was directing our attention to who we were as opposed to who we were supposed to be and what we were supposed to be doing.

"My mother never played with me. I did everything with my father. We'd go to the hardware store together and then to the gas station and then get a hot dog. My mother took me to pediatricians, the orthodontist, the eye doctor".

"You have trouble with your eyes?"

"I can't see anything without glasses. I have to feel around for my glasses when I wake up. I wear contacts but they don't feel right."

"I have the feeling you don't feel anyone sees you accurately."

"How do you know that?"

"I don't know, it just seems that way."

"You know, I'm older than I look. I'm 22."

"You're both older and younger than your age."

"I don't feel like I'm any age."

In the part of the session I have just described, Ms. V communicated with me from the moment I entered the waiting room when she looked pleadingly at me, seeming to be asking me to tell her how she should be with me. The unfashionable way she dressed commanded attention. In the consulting room, she told me about other ways she had of attempting to be seen: her not following instructions in her doctoral program, her insulting customers at the clothing store, and her playing nurse on her father's hospital rounds.

In this early part of the session, Ms. V created a picture of her mother as a person who could not play with her and could not see who she was beyond her projections. The paradox at the core of the portion of the session I am presenting might be described as the patient needed me to be her unaccepting mother *and* the patient needed me to be myself. If I were experienced by the patient as either her mother or myself, it would not have been enough. I had to be experienced as her mother and as myself. I held no value for the patient if I was not one or both of her parents, and I held no value for her if I was not myself, a person with the capacity to see her, to recognize her, and to play with her.

Ms. V's questioning whether I thought her going on hospital rounds was acceptable reflected her confusion about how to determine if she was who her mother saw her to be or who her father saw her to be, neither of which had much to do with who she was. I had the feeling the patient and her father were engaged in a pathological form of playing in which her father's patients were being used as playthings, not as ill people with feelings and lives of their own. Ms. V seemed to want to be sure I had read all the books in my library, perhaps to ensure I knew what I was supposed to be doing, for example, in knowing how to be a doctor different from her father.

A significant moment in the session occurred when the patient told me I was old and then said that she is older than she looks. This seemed to me to be an effort on her part to help me better see who she is and an opportunity for me to provide her an experience of being recognized.

When I ask myself if Ms. V's efforts to be seen are conscious or unconscious, it seems to me that the concepts of the conscious and unconscious minds do not well describe my experience with her. She needed to be seen, to be recognized, neither of which is either a conscious or an unconscious phenomenon. Such needs lie at the "core of ourselves" (what might be called our soul). Is soul a conscious or an unconscious phenomenon? It doesn't make sense to me to ask this question.

At almost every turn in this session, I could have viewed what was happening from the perspective of the concept of the unconscious mind. I might have viewed her playing nurse with her father as an expression of oedipal love that had to be hidden from her mother, who was jealous of the patient when she accompanied her father on his rounds. I might have viewed her difficulty with her vision as a reflection of her fear of seeing conflictual aspects of her repressed unconscious. I might have viewed her failure to observe the rules of her doctoral program and her insulting the shoppers where she worked as expressions of unconscious anger, perhaps at her mother. So, one might ask, "What is the harm in making use of the concept of the unconscious in conceiving of things in this way and eventually making interpretations based on these inferences?" From my perspective, a problem with approaching the initial portion of this session from the perspective of the concept of the unconscious is that it fosters a state of mind in which one is attempting to arrive at understandings of unconscious meanings that lie below or beneath what is happening in the session. The concept of the unconscious frames what is happening in a session in a way that creates the illusion that there are answers to questions that need to be answered, and that the answers to one set of questions form the starting place for the search for answers to another set of questions that lie beneath them or behind them.

In the session I have described, I was engaged with Ms. V not primarily in an effort to understand her but in an effort to recognize her, to see her for who she was. The need to be seen by another person is necessary to one's gaining a sense of who one is. One cannot become anyone without being seen, beginning with the infant's experience of seeing himself or herself reflected in what the mother sees in the infant as she looks at him or her (Winnicott, 1967). The need to be seen is not a conscious or an unconscious wish, it is an existential need. In working with Ms. V, I was engaged not primarily in enhancing her self-understanding but in seeing her, recognizing her, and inviting her to play with me.[2]

In sum, the unconscious is an idea, a brilliant idea, but it is not a place or a second mind. The use of the idea of the unconscious mind is indispensable in making inferences about what is occurring in the (imaginary) "world" of unconscious internal object relationships. In response to the question, "Why not make use of the concept of the unconscious?" I would say that doing so in a consistent way is to become locked in a state of mind in which one is engaged in a search for answers to questions concerning latent meaning. To be engaged in a search for unconscious meaning may eclipse a state of mind in which one is concerned not with answering questions about unconscious meaning but with the patient's difficulty in coming into being as himself or herself, difficulty in experiencing himself or herself as real, not knowing who one is, feeling that one is nobody, and so on. Engaging in a search for understanding and engaging in generative experiences are two inseparable dimensions of psychoanalysis. Difficulty arises if one excludes the other. An excess of search for meaning (the epistemological dimension) may issue in an analysis that feels intellectual and dead; an excess of the analyst's investment in creating experiences in analysis in which the patient may come to feel more real and alive may issue in an analysis that feels unsafe and overwhelming to both patient and analyst (as occurred, for example, when Ferenczi allowed his "active technique" [1932, 1949] to become mutual analysis).

Concluding comment

Freud's (1900, 1915) concept of the unconscious lies at the core of my analytic thinking, but I am now keenly aware that there is no such entity as the unconscious. The unconscious does not exist as a second mind or as a part of an internal world split into conscious and unconscious parts. The unconscious is an idea, only an idea. From the perspective of an awareness that there is no such entity as the unconscious, I conceive of meaning being latent in consciousness (all we are able to experience: our thoughts, feelings, sensations, and experience of ourselves as both subject and object, I and me). In literature, meaning does not lie below the words or through the words, but in the words. So too, meaning does not lie under consciousness or behind it, but *in* consciousness, in the inferences we make about it. "There is another world, but it is in this one."

Notes

1 When I use the term "consciousness," I am referring to everything we are capable of experiencing: all of our thoughts, feelings, and sensations, and, as development proceeds, the capacity for self-reflection in which there is an "I" as subject and a "me" as object.

2 I have previously discussed (Ogden, 2019, 2020, 2023a, b) the interplay of what I call the "epistemological dimension of psychoanalysis" (having to do with coming to know and understand) and the "ontological dimension" (having to do with being and becoming). The former involves patient and analyst working to help the patient to achieve greater self-understanding; the latter draws on the experiences occurring in the analysis itself which contribute to patients becoming more fully themselves.

References

Eluard, P. (1968). *Oeuvres Completes*, Vol. 1. Paris: Galliamard, p. 986.

Ferenczi, S. (1932). *The Clinical Diary of Sandor Ferenczi*, ed. J. Dupont, trans. M. Balint & N. Jackson. Cambridge, MA: Harvard University Press, 1995.

Ferenczi, S. (1949). Confusion of the tongues between the adults and the child: The language of tenderness and of passion. *Int. J. Psychoanal.* 30: 225–230.

Freud, S. (1900). *The Complete Psychological Works of Sigmund Freud*, ed. J. Strachey. London: Hogarth Press, 1955.

Freud, S. (1915). *The Complete Psychological Works of Sigmund Freud*, ed. J. Strachey. London: Hogarth Press, 1955.

James, W. (1890). *Principles of Psychology,* ed. P. Smith, Vol. 1. New York: Dover, 1950.

Ogden, T. H. (2019). Ontological psychoanalysis, or what do you want to be when you grow up? *Psychoanal. Q.* 88: 661–684.

Ogden, T. H. (2020). Toward a revised form of analytic theory and practice: The evolution of analytic theory of mind. *Psychoanal. Q.* 89: 219–243.

Ogden, T. H. (2023). Like the belly of a bird breathing: On Winnicott's "Mind and its relation to psyche-soma." *Int. J. Psychoanal.* 101: 7–22.

Ogden, T. H. (2024). Ontological psychoanalysis in clinical practice. *Psychoanal. Q.* 93: 13–31.

Winnicott, D. W. (1949). Mind and its relation to psyche-soma. In *Through Paediatrics to Psycho-Analysis*. New York: Basic Books, 1950, pp. 243–254.

Winnicott, D. W. (1967). Mirror-role of mother and family in child development. In *Playing and Reality*. New York, NY: Basic Books, 1971, pp. 111–118.

4 Rethinking the concept of analytic time

I conceive of there being two inseparable sorts of experiences of time that stand in a dynamic relationship with one another. One sort of experience of time is "diachronic time" (from the Greek for "through" and "time"): "clock time" or "calendar time"; the other is "synchronic time" (from the Greek for "together" and "time"): "dream time." Diachronic time is sequential and closely associated with cause-and-effect logic. One experience follows another. A diachronic experience of time is being used when one says, "The supervisor caused J to feel embarrassed." One event follows from another; one period of life follows from another. Diachronic time is an experience in which there is separation of inside and outside, self and other. The internal and external are in a relationship of mutual influence; for example, the patient felt exposed by the analyst's ending the meeting in a way that felt abrupt, though she felt she may have been over-reacting. Patient and analyst work predominantly in a diachronic experience of time when the analyst ends the session on time or when the analyst notifies the patient of upcoming vacation dates. The patient, too, engages in a diachronic experience of time when she understands current experience in terms of childhood experience, when she arrives "on time" to her sessions, or when she leaves the consulting room at the end of a session without talking further to the analyst, and the like.

Developmental analytic theory relies on a diachronic conception of time: one period of life follows another, the oral stage is followed by the anal stage, adolescence follows latency, and the depressive position follows the paranoid-schizoid position.

I conceive of the synchronic experience of time as inseparable from a diachronic experience. Neither way of experiencing time exists in pure form. "Synchronic time" might be thought of as "dream time," time while playing, time while writing or painting, or time while being creative in some other way. While diachronic time is sequential, synchronic time is an experience of time in which all time is together in the present moment. As one dreams, all of time is together in dream time: "The past is not dead, it is not even past" (Faulkner, 1951). The present does not follow the past; all time is together in the present. It does not make sense to us to ask a patient how long his or her dream lasted. In the analytic session, the setting (the patient lying on the

DOI: 10.4324/9781003528821-5

couch, the analyst sitting behind the couch) is designed to help the patient let go of diachronic time, "clock time," and to enter a synchronic experience of time (dream time) in which patient and analyst engage in dreaming together the analytic session (Ogden, 2017). The patient coming into my consulting room and lying down on the couch, while I take my seat quietly behind the couch, always feels to me as if the patient and I are preparing to go to sleep and dream together.

From the vantage point of synchronic time, the past is gone, and it is irretrievable; one cannot go back to it; it is a memory. And yet, in synchronic time all of the past is in the present (as it is in dreaming). In the experience of synchronic time, the past is alive in the present in the form of the impressions that the past has left on the individual. In synchronic time, we are the totality of the experiences that have influenced us and have left their impression on us. This is the paradox of synchronic time: the past exists only as memory; and all of the past is alive in the present moment of who the individual is.

In synchronic time, time past is not continuous with time present, for they are different types of experiences of time. The past is gone and exists only as memory (thoughts and feelings) in the present: this is true of the events that occurred ten seconds ago and ten years ago. The present moment is "the present moment of the past" (Eliot, 1919, p. 11), the present moment informed by the impressions left on us by the entirety of our past experience.

In synchronic time, the past might be likened to the rings seen in the cross section of a tree in which annual growth and dormancy patterns are registered. The rings are not the past, but they are reflections of the past that are alive in the present moment of the living tree. The rings are not the experience they reflect. The rings are reflections of the tree's response to the past that is alive in the present moment of the tree.

From the perspective of synchronic time, the childhood traumatic event itself is gone but is alive in the present as a consequence of the impression it has left on the patient's present, evolving state of being who he or she is. The impression is alive in the very fiber of the being of the individual in the present moment; the impression is alive in what makes the individual who he or she is. The childhood trauma is alive in the impression left by the past on the patient. The trauma, as experienced in the analytic process, is not a memory of the past, but it is alive in the patient's very being and is experienced more fully in the co-created subjectivity of patient and analyst ("the analytic third," Ogden, 1994a, b).

From the perspective of synchronic time, the term *regression* is misleading in that it suggests that the patient returns to an earlier time, which is impossible because the past no longer exists, there is no past to return to. What occurs in analysis is the patient's coming into being in such a way that the impressions left on him or her by the past are lived with the analyst in the present. One is not "going back," but one is living in the analytic relationship the impression the past has left on the patient's way of being himself or herself. The experience of the trauma as lived in the analysis is an experience created for the first time by patient and analyst. What is created is not the traumatic experience that occurred in childhood, for that is gone. Nor is what is created a memory of what occurred. What is experienced is new to patient and analyst. The traumatic experience brought to life in the present moment of the analysis is a moment in which the patient is not alone with what she is experiencing as she was when the traumatic event occurred.

So too, the concept of the transference takes on different meaning when it is not viewed as the patient's projection of an internal object relationship onto the analytic relationship, and instead seen as the patient's living the present moment of the past from the perspective of the subjectivity co-created by patient and analyst.

Freud (1918) makes use of the perspective of synchronic time in his concept of "deferred action" (*Nachtraglichkeit*), a conception of the relationship of past and present in which the present was not experienced when it occurred. Freud's (1918) Wolf Man could not live the infantile experience of observing his parents' sexual intercourse when it occurred; he experienced it only later when he reached a stage of maturity when he was able to take in and respond to what occurred. The past did not occur until it was experienced in the present moment.

Winnicott (1974) conceives of childhood breakdown as a response to an event at which the individual was not able to be emotionally present because it was too painful or disorganizing for him or her to be there. The patient, in analysis, experiences fear of breaking down in the present, when the breakdown has already occurred in childhood. Because the childhood event was "unlived" (Ogden, 2014), the patient cannot learn from the experience. The analytic relationship is the setting in which what occurred may be experienced for the first time and integrated into the patient's ever-evolving experience of self.

Bion (1967) makes use of the concept of synchronic time when he says that the analyst must not concern himself or herself with memory of the past or with desire for what will occur in the future: "Memory and desire... deal respectively with sense impressions of what is supposed to have happened and sense impressions of what has not yet happened" (p. 136). Intrinsic to Bion's view of the past, present, and future is a synchronic conception of time: the past is dead (now, merely an idea about what is supposed to have happened), nor does the future exist (ideas about what we desire to happen); we exist only *in* the present. In the spirit of Paul Eluard's (1968) statement, "There is another world, but it is in this one," I would rephrase Bion by saying: "the past and future are other worlds, but they are in this one."

In the analytic setting, a patient having been sexually molested as a child need not be remembered in adulthood for it to have occurred. It is alive in the impression it has left on the patient and the impression the patient is making on the analyst, and on the experience the two are creating in the present moment of the analysis. When a patient tells me he or she has been sexually molested as a child, I do not rely on the patient's memory of the event to give me a sense that the molestation did indeed occur. The sexual molestation exists in the present in the form of the impressions those experiences have left on the very being of the patient and are communicated to me in the way the patient is with me, and in the experience the two of us are creating *now*. The effects of the childhood sexual molestation limit the patient and leave him or her with a "scarring" (the shutdown of becoming) that obstructs healthy psychic and somatic growth. We cannot change the past, but we can help shape the patient's "present moment of the past" as we live with the patient what the patient could not experience when the past events occurred.

Clinical illustration

When M. C began analysis, she said that she "did not feel herself." She felt like "a visitor" in her life. She tried to pick up clues from others about how to behave as a mother and wife. From the very beginning of the analysis, she relied on me to help her get "from one day to the next," and at the same time, she thoroughly mistrusted me. Though the weekend breaks were a torture for her, when with me she showered me with criticism; for example, she countered virtually everything I said by telling me that I was being judgmental or condescending or dense or uneducated. Ms. C would arrive about 15 minutes before her sessions. At the beginning of one of our sessions, she told me that I had been early in meeting her in the waiting room. She said, "Please begin the sessions on time, otherwise I don't know where I am."

In the course of the analysis, the patient began to trust me sufficiently to tell me about the sexual molestations she had experienced at the hands of an uncle, which lasted for years. Ms. C's accounts might be called memories, but I viewed them as our co-constructions that derived from the patient's internal reality. Linking these co-constructions with historical "facts" was of little interest to me because whatever those facts might have been, they no longer existed except in the impressions the experiences had made on the patient. As the patient described what she remembered of the molestations, I pictured the rooms in which these events occurred in such vivid detail that at times I forgot that these were my own imaginings.

In the course of years of analysis, Ms. C began to be able to accept that there was nothing she could do to make the memories of the molestations "disappear" or make the events "unhappen." Ms. C became far less angry at me and better able to feel compassion for herself as a child and at present. One day, she said, "Until now I've had the feeling that 'we've' been doing this analysis together, but now there's no 'we,' I'm on my own." I responded, "It's true you alone feel the pain in your life, but it's important to both of us that I know about it."

In what I have described in the work with Ms. C, one can see the interplay of diachronic and synchronic experiences of time and the way in which both were essential. The patient was adamant that diachronic time be honored (she demanded that I adhere precisely to the time we agreed to start the sessions) because my not adhering to the agreed-upon starting time led her to feel she could not "know where I am." She was beseeching me not to undermine her efforts to hold onto who she is in the experience of the sexual molestation as it was being lived in the analysis.

Toward the end of the period of analysis I have described, Ms. C said that there used to be a "we," but now no longer. Her feeling that she was utterly alone now seemed to me to reflect a passage from her experiencing the childhood trauma (predominantly) from the perspective of a co-created subjectivity (in a synchronic experience of time) to experiencing the feeling of being alone with her pain and being separate from me, both of which reflect a diachronic experience of time. My response to the patient—"It's true you alone feel the pain in your life, but it's important to both of us that I know about it"—was my way of telling her that her experience of the sexual molestation is hers alone, but it was important to both of us that I know about the experience and be with her as she makes it her own. Implicit in what I said was my feeling that I was a person separate from the patient, which was essential if I was to be able to "bear witness" (Poland, 2000) to her having suffered sexual molestations in childhood and her continuing to experience their aftereffects.

Concluding comment

The experience of time in the analytic session is at once synchronic (from the Greek for "together" and "time") and diachronic (from the Greek for "through" and "time"). In synchronic experience of time, all time exists in the present moment in the form of the impression that the past has left on who we are. The patient who brings trauma to the analysis needs the analyst to co-create and live the experience of the trauma with the patient (in synchronic time), an experience in which the patient is not alone, and at the same time, the patient needs the analyst to be a separate person who is able to bear witness to his or her experience of childhood traumatic events and their sequelae (in diachronic time).

References

Bion, W. R. (1967). Notes on memory and desire. In *Wilfred Bion: Los Angeles Seminars and Supervision*, ed. J. Aguayo & B. Malin. London: Karnac, 2013, pp. 136–138.
Eliot, T. S. (1919). Tradition and individual talent. In *Selected Essays*. New York: Harcourt, Brace, and World, 1960, pp. 3–11.
Eluard, P. (1968). *Oeuvres Completes*, Vol. 1. Paris: Galliamard, p. 986.
Faulkner, W. (1951). *Requiem for a Nun*. New York: Random House.
Freud, S. (1918). From the history of an infantile neurosis. *SE* 17. London: Hogarth Press, 1955, vol. 88, pp. 681–684.
Ogden, T. H. (1994a). The analytic third: Working with intersubjective clinical facts. *Int. J. Psychoanal.* 75: 3–20.
Ogden, T. H. (1994b). *Subjects of Analysis*. Northvale, NJ: Jason Aronson.

Ogden, T. H. (2014). Fear of breakdown and the unlived life. *Int. J. Psychoanal.* 91: 205–224.

Ogden, T. H. (2017). Dreaming the analytic session: A clinical essay. *Psychoanal. Q.* 86: 1–20.

Poland, W. (2000). The analyst's witnessing and otherness. *J. Am. Psychoanal. Assn.* 48: 80–93.

Winnicott, D. W. (1967) Mirror-role of mother and family in child development. In *Playing and Reality.* New York: Basic Books, 1971, pp. 111–118.

5 Giving back what the patient brings

On Winnicott's "Mirror-role of mother and family in child development"

Winnicott's (1967) "Mirror-role of mother and family in child development" is, to my mind, one of his most important contributions concerning the formation of the experience of self. In it, Winnicott presents his understanding of the infant's coming into being as he sees himself reflected in the eyes of the mother.

What the mother sees there

Winnicott begins the paper: "In individual emotional development *the precursor of the mirror is the mother's face*" (p. 111, italics in original). He will devote the rest of the paper to fleshing out this idea.

Winnicott states for himself and the reader the framework of his thinking concerning early development:

> The bare statement is this: in the early stages of the emotional development of the human infant a vital part is played by the environment which in fact is not yet separated off from the infant by the infant. Gradually the separating-off of the not-me from the me takes place. The major changes take place in the separating-out of the mother as an objectively perceived environmental feature.
>
> (p. 111)

The mother (the environment) and the infant, early on, are engaged in a process through which the environment develops from a state in which the mother is not a separate person to a state in which the infant is able to see the mother as separate from himself. The subject is created at the same moment as the object is created, for there cannot be a subject without an object or an object without a subject.

At the beginning:

> A baby is held, and handled satisfactorily, and with this taken for granted, is presented with an object in such a way that the baby's legitimate experience of omnipotence is not violated. The result can be that the

DOI: 10.4324/9781003528821-6

baby is able to use the object, and to feel as if this object is a subjective object, and created by the baby.

(p. 112)

This is a period of illusion. The mother is not yet a separate object (she is experienced as a *subjective object,* an extension of the infant). Only later is the infant "able to use the object" as a real person separate from himself (an *object objectively perceived*).

Having briefly described the infant's experience of the illusion of om- nipotence followed by gradual disillusionment, Winnicott asks, "What does the infant see when he or she first looks at the mother as a separate person?":

Now, at some point the baby takes a look round. Perhaps a baby at the breast does not look at the breast. Looking at the face is more likely to be a feature (Gough, 1962). What does the baby see there? To get to the answer we must draw on our experience with psychoanalytic patients who reach back to very early phenomena and yet who can verbalize (when they feel they can do so) without insulting the delicacy of what is preverbal, unverbalized, and unverbalizable except perhaps in poetry.

(p. 112)

It is surprising to me that Winnicott says that he relies on work with analytic patients to answer his question about what the baby sees when he first looks at the mother. He does not seem to turn to his work with the many hundreds of mothers and infants he has seen in his work as a pediatrician, which con- tinued until the very end of his life. I suppose Winnicott would say that his pa- tients are able, at times, to experience with him and tell him something about their internal experience when in a regressed state. By contrast, infants—who are, by definition, preverbal—are not able to describe their subjective experi- ence. I differ from Winnicott here for I have experienced with my own chil- dren when they were infants psychic states elicited in me that seemed to be rather specific communications by the infant of his own psychic state. (James Grotstein told me that English was his second language. I was startled be- cause I had known him for 25 years and never had a clue this was so. I asked what his first language was. He said, "Baby talk.")

Winnicott in the space of three sentences now presents the central point of his paper:

What does the baby see when he or she looks at the mother's face? I am suggesting that, ordinarily, what the baby sees is himself or herself. In other words the mother is looking at the baby and *what* she looks like is related to *what* she sees there.

(p. 112, italics in original)

In the second of these sentences, Winnicott states that what the infant sees in the mother's face is himself or herself. He modifies this idea in the sentence that follows: "*what* she [the mother] looks like is related to *what* she sees there." In this second sentence, two crucially important conditionals are introduced. The infant sees something *like* himself and something *related to* himself. These conditionals open a space in which imaginative thinking may occur for both the infant and the mother. The infant is not seeing a mirror-image of himself for such an image is mechanical and lifeless. What the infant sees is the mother's creation, her physical and emotional response to what she sees in her infant. The mother, in health, is able to see and take pleasure in who her infant is.

There is an implicit paradox here. The mother creates the infant (in her subjective response to the infant, a creation that is unique to her), and the mother objectively discovers the infant (in recognizing all that is unique to him or her, which she could not have invented). The question, "Does the mother create or discover the infant?" is not to be asked, just as one must not ask a child if the fire truck he is playing with is real or imaginary. The mirroring experience of mother and infant is a form of playing. One must not solve the paradox. Winnicott asks that the paradox underlying playing and mirroring and all imaginative life be "accepted and tolerated and accepted, and for it not to be resolved" (Winnicott, 1971, p. xii).

In a sense, the mother must *know nothing* as she looks at and responds to her infant, for knowing in advance is the mother's projection, not a response to who the infant is. In this spirit, Winnicott (1969) says that in his analytic work, he interprets "mainly to let the patient know the limits of my understanding" (pp. 86–87), the limits of what he knows.

Failure of recognition

An individual cannot grow up in a healthy way without another person whose responses help her see who she is. In the absence of the response of the mother and others, the infant experiences herself as no one, or as an imitation of a person, or the person her mother needs her to be, or some other substitute for the experience of being seen as uniquely herself.

Winnicott is by no means naïve concerning the difficulty a mother may have in communicating her response to the infant.

> I am asking that this which is naturally done well by mothers who are caring for their babies shall not be taken for granted. I can make my point by going straight over to the case of the baby whose mother reflects her own mood or, worse still, the rigidity of her own defences. In such a case what does the baby see?
>
> (p. 112)

There are easy babies and difficult babies, babies that take instant delight in the mother and the world, and babies who find the world too much for them, for it is too noisy, too bright, and too much. The difficult babies often have trouble nursing or sleeping or molding to the shape of the mother. The face of a mother of an inconsolable infant is likely to reflect worry, not only about what is troubling her infant but also about her ability to be a mother to this infant or to be a mother at all. Under such circumstances, the question is not only "What does the baby see in the mother's face?" but also "What does the mother see in the infant's face?"

Winnicott goes on to say, "Of course nothing can be said about the single occasions on which the mother could not respond. Many babies, however, do have a long experience of not getting back what they are giving" (p. 112). I am struck by the wording of the second sentence. Winnicott, here, views the infant not only as a passive agent to whom care and love are given, but also as an active agent who is *giving* to the mother his or her love, tenderness, molding, and a look of recognition in his eyes. This giving is sustaining of the mother when she sees in his eyes *what he sees there in her*. There is no such thing as a baby in the absence of a mother (Winnicott, 1960), and I would add that there is no such thing as a mother in the absence of a baby.

The effect of the mother's experience of seeing herself as a mother in the eyes of the infant comes forcefully into view when the infant is in chronic distress, for example, a colicky baby, a sickly baby, and a baby unable to sleep for more than an hour. The mother of such infants sees in the eyes of her baby a mother who is inadequate. The infant clamoring for relief from pain demands omnipotence of the mother, the power to relieve him of his pain if she chooses to. The mother, too, demands of herself omnipotence which she is unable to provide and in that sense is a failure. In health, mothers and infants create experiences of mutual recognition together, seeing themselves reflected in the eyes of the other; the disruption of this experience of mutual recognition is devastating for both mother and infant. In "Hate in the countertransference," Winnicott (1949) comments on the experience of the mother whose infant makes her feel like a failure. She hates the baby because she feels: "If she fails him at the start she knows he will pay her out forever" (p. 201). I would add that the mother does an even better job than the infant of paying herself out for her "failure" as a mother, even if her failure is a failure to be omnipotent.

Winnicott describes two *consequences* of the mother's inability to reflect what she sees there in the infant: "First, their [the infants'] own creative capacity begins to atrophy, and in some way or other they look around for other ways of getting something of themselves back from the environment" (p. 112). For Winnicott, being alive is a "creative" activity; in being alive (as opposed to surviving), one is all the time imaginatively creating oneself. In part, this takes place in the medium of others' responses to oneself. In the absence of the experience of being recognized, the infant's capacity to see creatively atrophies; the world becomes dull or confusing.

In reading this passage about the atrophy of the infant's creative capacity, I am reminded of G, a psychotic adolescent with whom I worked for three years on a long-term inpatient unit. Among G's symptoms was his habit of walking endlessly around the neighborhood in which he grew up, and when feeling like a nap, entering any house he happened to be near, finding a bedroom, getting into bed, and going to sleep. Every bed was interchangeable with any other bed.

In the five-session-per-week work with G, there developed a period in which he related to me only by imitating every bodily movement I made, every word I spoke, every expression on my face, and every posture I took. His relentless imitation drained me of my sense of who I was. I could feel myself disappearing, becoming nobody (no body). Over time, I came to understand G's imitation of me as a communication of his experience of looking into his severely disturbed mother's eyes, where he saw not life, not an imaginative response to what she saw there in him, but instead saw a deadened and deadening imitation of life, imitation of being a mother, and imitation of being a person. Everything was interchangeable with everything else. Nothing held personal meaning. He was everyone and no one to her, a being who existed only as an imitation of life.

The two-way process of seeing and being seen

Winnicott, in discussing the consequences of the mother's inability to express to the infant what she sees there, writes:

> The baby gets settled in to the idea that when he or she looks, what is seen is the mother's face [not a response to himself]. The mother's face is not then a mirror. So perception takes the place of apperception, perception takes the place of that which might have been the beginning of a significant exchange with the world, a two-way process in which self-enrichment alternates with the discovery of meaning in the world of seen things.
>
> (pp. 112–113)

Some infants do not see in their mother's face her response to him or her, but instead a response to the mother's own worries, fears, depression, confusion, and preoccupations. "The mother's face is not then a mirror." Under such circumstances, perception (sensory registration of what is seen) replaces apperception (making sense of new experience by integrating it into the structure of understandings of experience one already has and doing something of one's own with the new experience).

Apperception, as Winnicott is using the term, is not only a form of receptivity but also a form of communication—"a two-way process in which self-enrichment alternates with the discovery of meaning in the world of seen things." The infant's experience of seeing something like himself reflected in his mother's eyes is formative of the infant's experience of self, and the experience of self underlies his or her ability to discover and create meaning in all that he or she sees (including the mother).

Winnicott describes ways the infant responds when unable to see himself or herself in the eyes of the mother: "Some babies do not quite give up hope and they study the object and do all that is possible to see in the object some meaning that ought to be there if only it could be felt" (p. 113). These infants are searching for an affirmation of a sense of self that is beginning to form but cannot consolidate without affirmation gained by the mother's creative reflection of the infant. One cannot become oneself without another person's response to who one is.

Other babies, Winnicott tells us, who are

> … tantalized by this type of relative maternal failure, study the variable maternal visage in an attempt to predict the mother's mood, just exactly as we all study the weather. The baby quickly learns to make a forecast: "Just now it is safe to forget the mother's mood and to be spontaneous, but any minute the mother's face will become fixed or her mood will dominate, and my own personal needs must then be withdrawn, otherwise my central self may suffer insult."
>
> (p. 113)

Winnicott is describing the infant attempting to find in the fluctuating expression on the mother's face an indication of when it may be safe to look there for a reflection of who he or she is, but finding that this opportunity never occurs.

Winnicott continues this line of thought:

> Immediately beyond this in the direction of pathology is predictability, which is precarious, and which strains the baby to the limits of his or her capacity to allow for events. This brings a threat of chaos, and the baby will organize withdrawal, or will not look except to perceive [merely register sensory input], as a defence. A baby so treated will grow up puzzled about mirrors and what the mirror has to offer. If the mother's face is unresponsive, then a mirror is a thing to be looked at but not to be looked into.
>
> (p. 113)

The infant, in an effort to control the uncontrollable look on his mother's face, attempts to seize ownership of the mother's face by projecting onto it his own state of mind. This momentarily creates the illusion that the infant has made the mother's face predictable, but this effort is doomed and renders the infant unable to "allow for events," that is, to take life as it comes, to do something creative with one's personal response to life events. The divide between this sort of infant's projections and the real events of life is so great as to render the world chaotic, utterly ununderstandable. In response to the chaos and confusion the infant experiences, the infant has no recourse but to "organize withdrawal" from the world, that is, to create an organized defensive structure (perhaps schizoid [Fairbairn 1944] or autistic [Tustin 1981] in nature). An infant who grows up in this way "will grow up puzzled about mirrors and what the mirror has to offer," that is, the individual will have no sense of the value of seeing his reflection in someone else's eyes. One will see the mirroring that others do not as a way of discerning who one is, but as an event to merely perceive (to register sensorially) without being able to do anything with it (to apperceive), to look into it and into oneself.

Use of mirrors in health

Winnicott now turns to healthy children engaged with mirrors: "[W]hen the average girl studies her face in the mirror she is reassuring herself that the mother-image is there and that the mother can see her and that the mother is *en rapport* with her" (p. 113). "The average girl" who looks at her face in the mirror sees in the mirror the presence of her mother who is *"en rapport"* with her. The phrase *en rapport* has at least three meanings in French that include "to yield," "to carry in," and "to carry back." It seems to me that Winnicott is making use of all three of these meanings when he describes the relationship of the girl to her mother whom she is seeing in the mirror. The girl *yields to her mother* as her mother recognizes, responds to her, and sees who she is; she allows herself to be *carried by her mother,* as the look in her eyes seems to fold the girl in her arms and transport her to a more defined sense of herself; and the mother helps the girl *carry back into herself* what she has seen reflected in her mother's eyes.

As I read the sentence that follows, I am puzzled at first: "[W]hen girls and boys in their secondary narcissism look in order to see beauty and to fall in love, there is already evidence that doubt has crept in about their mother's continued love and care" (p. 113). Initially, I see nothing wrong with girls and boys searching for beauty and wanting to fall in love. I wonder why Winnicott sees such desires as reflections of their doubt concerning their mothers' love.

Winnicott responds: "So the man who falls in love with beauty is quite different from the man who loves a girl and feels she is beautiful and can see what is beautiful about her" (p. 113). The man who falls in love with beauty wants to find beauty in himself because he did not have the experience of feeling beautiful to his mother when he was an infant. He searches in vain for the reflection in his mother's eyes of what she sees of him and what she finds beautiful in him.

How different this man is from "the man who loves a girl and feels she is beautiful and can see what is beautiful about her." This man falls in love with the girl, not with himself, and he sees what is beautiful about her, not what is beautiful about himself.

The two sentences I have just quoted are the coda of the theoretical part of Winnicott's paper.

Clinical illustrations

About two-thirds of Winnicott's paper is devoted to clinical illustrations. Winnicott opens the clinical portion of his paper by saying, "I will not try to press home my idea, but instead I will give some examples so that the idea I am presenting can be worked over by the reader" (p. 113). I find in this sentence an essence of Winnicott. He does not provide the reader elements of an ideology that he espouses; he offers the reader something with which the reader may be able to make something of his or her own. This is Winnicott's style as a writer and as a practicing analyst.

Illustration I

The first clinical illustration is quite odd. It is only a page long. At first, it seems not to illustrate very much clinically. The person who is the subject of the account is not a patient, she is an "acquaintance" (p. 113). The story Winnicott tells begins, "I refer first to a woman of my acquaintance who married and brought up three fine male children" (p. 113). The sentence seems to adopt a misogynistic conventional belief that there is little more a woman can hope to achieve than to bring up three fine boys. It is difficult to imagine that Winnicott does not hear the irony in what he is saying.

Winnicott then creates a visual image in which we are told something about the interior life of this woman: "Behind the scenes this woman was always near to depression" (p. 113). This posed a difficulty not only for herself but also for her husband: "She seriously disturbed her marital life by waking every morning in a state of despair" (p. 113).

Winnicott tells us, "The resolution of the paralyzing depression came each day when at last it was time to get up, and at the end of her ablutions and dressing, she 'put on her face'" (p. 114). The woman found "resolution" to her depression when she "put on her face." Again, the tone is ironic: putting on her face is hardly a "resolution" of depression. Winnicott concludes this single-paragraph description with a terse statement about the fate of this woman: "This exceptionally intelligent and responsible person did eventually react to a misfortune by developing a chronic depressive state which in the end became transformed into a chronic and crippling physical disorder" (p. 114).

Winnicott comments, "What is illustrated by this case only exaggerates that which is normal. The exaggeration is of the task of getting the mirror to notice and approve. The woman had to be her own mother" (p. 114). This woman, Winnicott speculates, did not have an experience with her mother in which she found something of herself reflected in her mother's eyes. The face she "put on" in the morning is an inhuman face, the inanimate face she saw in her mother's eyes.

Winnicott closes his discussion of the first clinical illustration with three enigmatic statements that are like a poem in that they do not yield to paraphrase. Nonetheless, it is left to each of us to do what we can with these sentences:

When I look I am seen, so I exist.

(p. 114)

In a single clause—"when I look I am seen"—the experiences of seeing and being seen become a single mutually enriching experience of subject and object. This mutually enriching experience of looking and being seen underlies coming into being. The "I" in "so I exist" is different from the two "I's" in the first clause, in that the "I" in "so I exist" carries a feeling of having arrived at a psychic place not experienced before.

Winnicott's second thought in this series of three:

> I can now afford to look and see.
>
> (p. 114)

Having been seen as an infant gives one the freedom to genuinely see another person because seeing does not fill one with the feeling of not having been seen.

His concluding thought:

> I now look creatively and what I apperceive I also perceive.
>   In fact I take care not to see what is not there to be seen (unless I am tired).
>
> (p. 114)

In seeing another person creatively, one is both drawing on one's personal way of creating meaning (apperceiving) and attending closely to who the other person is (perceiving). One must be sure that one is not simply inventing the other person on the basis of one's own projections and other defenses. "I take care not to see what is not there." Tacking on "(unless I am tired)" serves as a reminder that one is only human.

Illustration II

Winnicott introduces us to a patient with a "striking appearance" (p. 115) who could be the "central figure of any group" (p. 115) if she were able to "use herself" (p. 115). She tells Winnicott about having been to a coffee bar with a man. Winnicott asks, "Did anyone look at you?" (p. 115). She tells him that the man she was with drew the attention from her.

Winnicott does not go into detail about this woman's childhood. He merely says that she had "a deplorable history" (p. 115). The whole analysis revolved around "her 'being seen' for what she in fact is" (p. 115). This one-sentence *case history and course of treatment* would ordinarily leave the reader feeling he or she needs to hear more. But this is a sketch, not a portrait. He says merely, "at times the being actually seen in a subtle way is for her the main thing in her treatment" (p. 115). *The experience of being seen,* not the expansion of the patient's self-understanding, is what is important in this analysis.

Winnicott closes this brief half-page clinical illustration: "This patient is particularly sensitive as a judge of painting and indeed of the visual arts, and lack of beauty disintegrates her personality so that she recognizes lack of beauty by herself feeling awful (disintegrated or depersonalized)" (p. 115). The focus here is not on the patient's response to beauty but on her response to "lack of beauty," which makes her feel "awful." Lack of beauty in visual art seems to cause the patient to feel identified with what is *not* worth looking at, *not* worth seeing, *unworthy* of being seen. This tears her apart and causes her to experience a lack of internal cohesiveness.

In this and other illustrations, Winnicott shows us his style as an analyst, which is to be distinguished from his technique. Technique is a set of principles passed down from one generation of analysts to the next which guide the analyst's method of working with patients. By contrast, style is the analyst's unique way of being with patients that reflects the totality of who he is, the life he has lived, the experiences with patients he has had, and so on (Ogden, 2007). Another analyst's style is to be appreciated, not imitated.

Clinical illustration III

In a little over a page, Winnicott describes an analysis that revolved around "the effect on [the patient] of her depressed mother" (p. 115). He says he "had to displace the mother in a big way in order to enable the patient to get started as a person" (p. 115). Winnicott introduces his own theory of depression and its treatment here: depression is the outcome of the patient's taking in the mother's depression in an effort to relieve the mother of that pain. It is necessary for Winnicott to "displace the mother in a big way." Winnicott's use of the word "displace" seems to suggest an experience in analysis in which Winnicott is someone decidedly different from the mother.

Winnicott says of the patient's use of mirrors:

> This patient has a marked absence of that which characterizes so many women, an interest in the face… now she looks in the mirror only to remind herself that "she looks like an old hag" (patient's own words).
>
> (pp. 115–116)

Perhaps the patient looks in the mirror only to remind herself she is an old hag because seeing herself as an old hag is better than not being seen at all.

The patient asked Winnicott to send her a portrait of himself.

> [She] thought that she was quite simply acquiring the portrait of this man who had done so much for her (and I have). But what she needed to be told was that my lined face had some features that link for her with the rigidity of the faces of her [depressed] mother and her nurse.
>
> (p. 116)

Winnicott adds:

> I feel sure that it was important that I knew this about the face [the link between the lines on his face and those on the faces of her mother and

nurse], and that I could interpret the patient's search for a face that could reflect herself, and at the same time see that, because of the lines, my face in the picture reproduced some of her mother's rigidity.

(p. 116)

It was necessary for the patient to find in Winnicott "a face that could reflect herself." But Winnicott, at the same time, had to be, for this patient, her mother in all of her rigidity. One or the other would not have been enough. This experience, with its strong ties to the past (her mother) and to the present (the experience with Winnicott), may be what Winnicott has in mind when he says he had to "displace" the mother. He had to be the mother at the same time as he was being himself. This is a central paradox of analytic treatment: the analyst being the transference object and the analyst not being the transference object.

He ends the clinical illustration:

Actually the patient has a thoroughly good face, and she is an exceptionally sympathetic person when she feels like it...The fact is, however, that the moment my patient feels herself being involved, especially in someone's depression, she automatically withdraws and curls up in bed with a hot water bottle, nursing her soul. Just here she is vulnerable.

(p. 116)

In commenting that the patient has a "thoroughly good face," Winnicott is once again breaking the rules of writing analytic essays. Winnicott's narrative voice is informal and expressive of personal feeling: he likes this woman's face, he likes this woman, and he reflects this in his response to her. He sees the patient as she is, including her intolerance of depression in others and her need to take to bed when exposed to others' depression. Winnicott is able to recognize and accept—perhaps even love—the patient in her vulnerability, in her entirety.

Illustration IV

Winnicott begins the fourth clinical illustration: "After all this had been written a patient brought material in an analytic hour which might have been based on this that I am writing" (p. 116). At the juncture in the analysis that Winnicott is describing, he was engaged in writing this paper on the infant's coming into being as he or she sees himself or herself reflected in the eyes of the mother. It is unclear whether Winnicott is aware that he is illustrating a way in which his patient was creatively mirroring him, recognizing him for who he was at the present moment. I view the patient's recognition of Winnicott as part of the mutual recognition that is intrinsic to an analysis that is going well. I would be surprised if Winnicott was not leaving room for the reader to discover what he or she might.

In this final clinical illustration, Winnicott does nothing less than lay out the foundations of his theory of the mutative factors in the practice of psychoanalysis and the ways the analyst facilitates this aspect of the analytic process. He describes a patient whose mother, when the patient was an infant, was "talking to someone else unless actively engaged in a positive relating to the baby… the baby would look at the mother and see her talking to someone else" (pp. 116–117).

In a session, the patient spoke about Francis Bacon's preference for having his paintings framed under glass so the viewers see not only the painting but also themselves reflected in the glass. The patient went on to comment on Lacan's "Le Stad du Miroir," but "she was not able to make the link that I feel I am able to make between the mirror and the mother's face" (p. 117).

> It was not my job to give this link to my patient in this session because the patient is essentially at a stage of discovering things for herself, and premature interpretation in such circumstances annihilates the creativity of the patient and is traumatic in the sense of being against the maturational process… Psychotherapy is not making clever and apt interpretations; by and large it is a long-term giving the patient back what the patient brings.
>
> (p. 117)

What we are doing as analysts is not making "clever and apt" interpretations of what is going on unconsciously for the patient; rather, our task is that of "long-term giving back what the patient brings," that is, reflecting what the analyst "sees there" in the patient.

Winnicott goes on to state his conception of the aim of psychoanalysis. There are few places in Winnicott's writings where he manages to convey the essence of his entire project as well as he does in this passage and the one I have quoted immediately above:

> [I]f I do this [desist from making clever interpretations] well enough the patient will find his or her own self, and will be able to exist and to feel real. Feeling real is more than existing; it is finding a way to exist as oneself, and to relate to objects as oneself, and to have a self into which to retreat for relaxation.
>
> (p. 117)

In these two passages, we can see the revolutionary nature of Winnicott's contribution to psychoanalysis. The language we use to describe what we do as analysts and what we have as our goals has changed from the language of making the unconscious conscious and resolving unconscious conflict. For these formulations, Winnicott substitutes the idea that the analyst's role involves not making clever interpretations and instead protecting the patient's need and right to creatively make his or her own discoveries and, in the experience of the joy of discovering for oneself, to feel real and alive. It is the role of the analyst to get out of the way as the patient discovers what the analyst may have known for some time. In protecting the patient's need to make his or her own discoveries, the analyst is safeguarding not only the value of the discoveries made, he is, more importantly, safeguarding the patient's experience of discovering.

References

Fairbairn, W. R. D. (1944). Endopsychic structures considered in terms of object-relationships. In *Psychoanalytic Studies of the Personality*. London: Routledge & Kegan Paul, 1952, pp. 82–132.

Gough, D. (1962). The behaviour of infants in the first year of life. *Proc. Roy. Soc. Med.*, 55.

Ogden, T. H. (2007). Elements of analytic style: Bion's clinical seminars. *Int. J. Psychoanal.* 88: 1185–1200.

Tustin, F. (1981). *Autistic States in Children*. Boston, MA: Routledge & Kegan Paul.

Winnicott, D. W. (1949). Hate in the countertransference. In *Through Pediatrics to Psycho-Analysis*. New York: Basic Books, 1975, pp. 194–203.

Winnicott, D. W. (1960). The theory of the parent-infant relationship. In *The Maturational Processes and the Facilitating Environment*. New York: International Univ. Press, 1965, pp. 166–170.

Winnicott, D. W. (1967). Mirror-role of mother and family in child development. In *Playing and Reality*. New York: Basic Books, 1971, pp. 111–118.

Winnicott, D. W. (1969). The use of an object and relating through identifications. In *Playing and Reality*. New York: Basic Books, pp. 86–94.

Winnicott, D. W. (1971). Introduction. In *Playing and Reality*. New York: Basic Books, pp. xi–xiii.

6 Like the belly of a bird breathing

On Winnicott's "Mind and its relation to the psyche-soma"

Winnicott's (1949) "Mind and its relation to the psyche-soma" is a very difficult paper about which I have delayed writing for more than 20 years. Only now, when I feel I have some sense of the multiplicity of meanings of psyche and soma, mind and body, imaginative self and alive body do I offer a reading of this paper. The meanings of these pairs of words in Winnicott's paper slip and slide into and out of one another, often leaving to the reader the task of making distinctions among them. It seems to me that Winnicott was thinking what he wrote (as opposed to writing what he thought) when he composed this paper and did not arrive at some of his ideas in their most fully developed form until the very end of the paper. As Winnicott's papers go, this is a long and tortuous one that often leads the reader to feel that he or she has lost track of the overall point of the paper, which is in fact a moving target.

This paper, to my mind, is one of Winnicott's most significant contributions. Here, he sets himself apart from both Melanie Klein and Freud who envision psychoanalysis as primarily epistemological, that is, having to do with coming to know and understand unconscious meaning. By contrast, Winnicott, in this paper, shifts the emphasis from the epistemological to the ontological dimension of psychoanalysis, that is, to the dimension having to do with being and becoming (see Ogden, 2019). While Klein and Freud focus, for example, on the unconscious meaning of play, Winnicott's interest, in this paper, is in the experience (the state of being) of playing (or breathing). Two years later, this shift in emphasis contributes to what is perhaps Winnicott's single most important contribution: the concept of transitional objects and phenomena (Winnicott, 1951), the imaginative space in which we live between fantasy and reality, and between discovering the object world and creating it.

In my "creative reading" of Winnicott's paper, I not only explicate and interpret his writing, I offer my own responses to the subjects at hand. When Winnicott leaves it to the reader to arrive at his or her own understandings, I will "write Winnicott" by fleshing out what I take to be implicit meaning.

I develop ideas that Winnicott only alludes to. Among these are (1) the idea that Winnicott works clinically by means of a combination of living an experience with the patient and bringing an unspoken system of meaning to the experience being lived in the session and (2) the idea that Winnicott introduces

DOI: 10.4324/9781003528821-7

a set of terms and a way of thinking that is independent of the differentiation of conscious and unconscious mind (Freud's topographic model). This set of terms and ideas includes the concepts of aliveness and deadness, realness and unrealness, continuity of being and disruption of continuity of being. These ideas do not replace the concepts of the conscious and unconscious mind, they offer a perspective that is operative alongside of the concepts of the conscious and unconscious mind.

Mind as a function of psyche-soma

Winnicott opens his paper by quoting a passage by Clifford Scott (1949) in which Scott states, "*I do not think that the mind really exists as an entity*" (Winnicott, 1949, p. 243, italics in original). Winnicott then states a guiding principle with which he will approach the question of mind: "To study the concept of mind one must always be studying an individual, a total individual, and including the development of that individual from the very beginning of psychosomatic existence" (p. 243). Winnicott, when studying human experience, always begins at the beginning.

When early development is satisfactory, "mind is then no more than a special case of the functioning of the psyche-soma" (p. 244). Mind, in health, is an expression not of psyche but of psyche-soma. "Mind," as Winnicott is using the term, is more verb than noun: it is an activity, an aspect of the *functioning* of the psyche-soma.

In establishing the language with which he is going to approach the topic of mind and psyche-soma, Winnicott says that the mental and the physical are not to be "opposed" (p. 244). He does not say here why this is the case except in the sense that mind and brain, activity and matter, should not be set against one another. He adds at the very end of the paper something that I am bringing to the beginning of my reading of the paper because I rely on the late clarification throughout my reading of the paper. He says at the end of the paper, "It is not logical ... to oppose the mental and the physical as these are not of the same stuff" (p. 254). This is a critical differentiation. The mental is *a form of experiencing* that is not located anywhere, while the physical is located in the body, which is a thing. The term *psyche* (as part of psyche-soma) refers to the *experience of being imaginatively alive* (which is not located anywhere). Soma is the *experience of physical aliveness,* which is not located anywhere, and is different from the body and the brain, which are things located somewhere.

The passage that immediately follows is, for me, one of the richest in Winnicott's paper in that it establishes the meaning of the concept of psyche-soma and why the mental and the physical are not to be opposed:

> Let us attempt, therefore, to think of the developing individual, starting at the beginning. Here is a body, and the psyche and the soma are not to be distinguished except according to the direction from which one is looking. One can look at the developing body or at the developing

psyche. I suppose the word psyche here means the *imaginative elaboration of somatic parts, feelings, and functions*, that is, of physical aliveness.

(p. 244, italics in the original)

In other words, at the outset of life there is the body and there is an as yet undifferentiated psyche and soma (psyche-soma is not *in* the body; it is a realm of experience different from that of the body, but related to it) "except according to the direction from which one is looking." Winnicott is imagining looking at the psyche-soma, an irreducible whole that is not localizable anywhere, from the perspective of psyche or from the perspective of soma. Looking at the psyche-soma from the perspective of psyche, "I suppose the word psyche here means the *imaginative elaboration of the somatic parts, feelings, and functions,* that is, of physical aliveness." I am always surprised by the final two words of this sentence: "physical aliveness." I anticipate that *psyche* means something that has to do with mental functioning. But psyche, for Winnicott, means mental functioning that imaginatively creates the experience of physical aliveness. Winnicott is using the experience of aliveness to define what it means for the psyche-soma to be healthy: aliveness of psyche is inseparable from aliveness of soma; psyche imaginatively creates the experience of physical aliveness. He concludes this paragraph by saying, "The psyche is not however, felt by the individual to be localized in the brain, or indeed to be localized anywhere" (p. 244). I would add: neither is soma (physical aliveness) located in the body or anywhere else.

In still other words, psyche is not to be confused with brain; and soma is not to be confused with body. This is a critical differentiation. Psyche-soma does not exist anywhere. Soma does not exist anywhere, not even in the body. The body is a thing; soma is an experience. Soma is the experience of physical aliveness; psyche is the experience of imaginative aliveness. Psyche-soma is not to be confused with mind-body; healthy psyche-soma could best be called the self. Winnicott is thinking while writing and is not quite ready this early in his thought process to make the differentiations I am making, but I find that making these distinctions is necessary to my thinking even in this very early part of the paper.

Winnicott seems to be leaning toward using verbs, not nouns, to describe the functioning of psyche-soma, but he does not quite arrive there. For instance, he uses the nouns "imaginative elaboration" instead of using the verbs and adverbs such as "imaginatively elaborating"; similarly, he uses the adjective and noun "physical aliveness" instead of using the verbs and adverbs "being physically alive" or "coming to life physically." I see the use of verbs in these instances as essential to Winnicott's argument, though he has not quite arrived there himself.

Winnicott further describes the development of psyche-soma:

Gradually the psyche and the soma aspects of the growing person become involved in a process of mutual interrelation. This interrelating of the psyche with the soma constitutes an early phase of individual development... At a later stage the live body, with its limits, and with an inside and an outside, is *felt by the individual* to form the core for the imaginative self.

(p. 244, italics in original)

It is the "live body," not the body that is *"felt by the individual* to form the core for the imaginative self." Winnicott is using the term *live body*, not *body*, because the "live body" is unlocalizable experience that is *"felt by the individual,"* while the body is a localizable thing. Just as physical aliveness is an imaginative elaboration of soma by psyche, psychic aliveness (the imaginative self) has for its core the experience of the "live body."

Theory of mind

The first part of this paper was about *the concepts of psyche and soma* from the very beginning of life and how they differ from the concepts of brain and body; this next section of the paper is about the development of the infant's *states of being* from the outset and how they relate to the development of psyche-soma:

Let us assume that health in the early development of the individual entails *continuity of being*. The early psyche-soma proceeds along a certain line of development provided *its continuity of being is not disturbed*; in other words, for the healthy development of the early psyche-soma there is a need for a *perfect* environment. At first the need is absolute.

(p. 245, italics in original)

Early development entails a great number of feeling states, but the one Winnicott prizes most in terms of the healthy development of psyche-soma is the experience of *continuity of being*. For continuity of being to be undisturbed, the environment must be "perfect" (p. 245). "At first the need is absolute" (p. 245). But I find myself protesting: perfection cannot be achieved by the mother; there are inevitable disturbances of the infant's "continuity of being," and these disturbances elicit defensive activity, the residues of which are inextricable parts of what makes us human. Winnicott, I believe, would agree, so why doesn't he say so? Why doesn't he use the term "near-perfect"? In response to these questions, I would point out that Winnicott is referring to the infant's "need for a perfect environment." But what the infant needs may not be what he always gets:

The perfect environment is one which *actively adapts* to the needs of the newly formed psyche-soma, that which we as observers know to be the infant at the start. A bad environment is bad because by failure to adapt it becomes an *impingement* to which the psyche-soma (i.e. the infant) must *react*. This reacting disturbs the continuity of the going-on-being of the new individual.

(p, 245, italics in original)

Going on being is a neologism (a verb without a subject). Winnicott is introducing this term as a way of describing the infant's subjectless state of being, for "there is no such thing as an infant" (Winnicott, 1960, p. 587, fn. 4) apart from the mother. The infant is not yet a subject; the mother holds the infant's subjectivity for him until he is ready to assume it.

Winnicott continues, "In its beginnings the good (psychological) environment is a physical one, with the child in the womb or being held and generally tended" (p. 245). For Winnicott, "holding" is not only the physical event of mother holding her infant in her arms; it is the emotional work the mother does in sustaining the infant's continuity of being.

Winnicott continues to flesh out the circumstances in which psyche-soma matures. Only with time and development does the infant's need for the perfect environment become relative, which allows the mother to become

the ordinary good mother with her ability to make adaptation to her infant's needs arising out of her devotion, made possible by her narcissism, her imagination, and her memories, which enable her to know through identification what are her baby's needs.

(p. 245)

The ordinary good mother is a person in her own right who makes use of her narcissism (her pride in, and control over, her infant). She is a product of her memories of her own infancy and childhood (real and imagined). And she "imagines her baby into existence" (Ogden, 2004a) (in a way that is both creative and limiting for the infant). It is these three emotional traits—narcissism, imagination, and memory—that enable the mother to identify with her infant and make use of these identifications to "know... what are her baby's needs." In this description of the ordinary good mother, Winnicott is describing a person with ordinary desires, needs, memories, strengths, and frailties, who uses her own experience to imagine herself into the place of the infant and come to know what he or she needs.

After a time, the infant (and the developing psyche-soma) no longer needs a perfect environment:

The *ordinary good mother is good enough*. If she is *good enough*, the infant becomes able to allow for her deficiencies by mental activity... even including the need for negative care or an alive neglect.

(p. 245, italics in original)

The infant is able to make use of "alive neglect," a term used, I think, to refer to the mother's allowing herself to "neglect" the infant (leave the infant on his own) while staying alive for him and to him. Winnicott, I think, is being playful in his use of the term *neglect* to refer to the mother's sensitive withdrawal as object while remaining alive as environment. This is part of what he later describes as the child's development of the capacity to be alone in the presence of the mother (Winnicott, 1958). "What releases the mother from her need to be near-perfect is the infant's understanding" (p. 245). "Understanding," I believe, refers to the infant's capacity to read the mother and be compassionate toward her when she attempts, but is not successful in, adapting to his needs. "The mental activity of the infant turns a *good enough* environment into a perfect one" (p. 245, italics in original). The infant's "mental activity" (psyche) is now able to make up for what the mother is not able to provide. There is now the infant and the mother in addition to the mother-infant.

The mother's role takes a turn at this point: "she tries to insulate her baby from coincidences and from other phenomena that must be beyond the infant's ability to comprehend" (p. 245). To my mind, the idea that the good enough mother "tries to insulate her baby from coincidences" refers to the mother's being aware that the infant will believe that his own feelings and behavior cause events to occur in the outside world. For instance, the infant may hold himself responsible for his mother's physical and emotional withdrawal or depression (perhaps, in response to an argument with her husband or the death of someone she loves) if the infant, by coincidence, is at the same time taking pleasure in his "muscle erotism" (Winnicott, 1952, p. 236) and his expression of "ruthless love" (Winnicott, 1947, p. 201) as he takes physical pleasure in his freedom to bite the nipple. To limit the impact of coincidences, "she keeps the world of the infant as simple as possible" (1949, p. 245). I read the phrase "as simple as possible" to mean the mother keeps the world in which she and the infant live as free as possible from the world external to the two of them and tries to keep her own responses to the infant understandable in the terms of the world they create and inhabit together.

Regarding the matters of mind and psyche-soma, Winnicott says:

> The mind, then, has as one of its roots a variable functioning of the psyche-soma, one concerned with the threat to continuity of being that follows any failure of (active) environmental adaptation. It follows that mind-development is very much influenced by factors not specifically personal to the individual, including chance events.
>
> (p. 246)

The term *mind* is being used to refer to an aspect of psyche-soma responsible for ("concerned with the threat to") continuity of being. Threats to continuity of being are caused by maternal failure of adaptation as well as chance events not personal to (having nothing to do with) the infant, such as, I imagine, the infant's physical illnesses, the grandfather's death, and the mother's response to the father's distress. Formerly, mind was "a special case of the functioning of psyche-soma," a healthy development of mental activities grounded in soma.

Here, mind includes a set of defensive reactions on the part of psyche-soma in response to threats to continuity of being.

We are now encountering a spate of terms used to refer to the mental and the physical, which are defined in large part by the way they are being used. For instance, regarding what is mental, there are the terms "psyche," "mind," "psyche-soma," "mental activity," "thinking," "understanding," "continuity of being," and "going on being"; and for the somatic there are the terms "body," "soma," "the physical," "alive body," and "physical aliveness." These will be, to some degree, sorted out by Winnicott, but the reader must tolerate a good deal of uncertainty, and in the end, many differentiations will be left for the reader to make.

Winnicott steps back at this point to reiterate an idea: "According to this theory [of mind] then, in the development of every individual, the mind has a root, perhaps its most important root, in the need of the individual, at the core of the self, for a perfect environment" (p. 246). This is the second time Winnicott refers to a "root" of the mind. The first time he mentioned that idea he said that mind has one of its roots in the reaction of psyche-soma to threats to continuity of being. The second "root" of the mind introduced here, "perhaps its most important root," is the need at the core of the self for a perfect environment. So, *mind* is rooted both in the infant's need for a perfect environment and in the defensive measures the infant takes in reaction to threats to going on being.

Winnicott clarifies his understanding of the relationship of the concepts "psyche, mind, and mental functioning":

> Certain kinds of failure on the part of the mother, especially erratic behaviour, produce over-activity of the [infant's] mental functioning. Here, in the over-growth of the mental function reactive to erratic mothering, we can see that there can develop an opposition between the mind and the psyche-soma, since in reaction to this abnormal environmental state the thinking of the individual begins to take over and organize the caring for the psyche-soma, whereas in health it is the function of the environment to do this.
>
> (p. 246)

Here, the term "mind" is being used to refer to an overactivity of mental functioning (excessive "thinking"), which stands in opposition to the psyche-soma. That is, it operates for purposes contrary to creating live body and imaginative self experience. "Mind" separates itself off from the experience of psyche-soma and establishes a new system of defenses that overthinks and segregates its activity from both psyche-soma and the mother's adaptations to the infant. Mind, under these circumstances, takes over the function of caring for the psyche-soma, a function that, in health, the mother provides. Thus, the mind operating in isolation from the mother and from the psyche-soma creates a closed loop in which the mind is insulated from anything outside itself and consequently cannot learn and cannot grow. The term *mind*, now, is no longer synonymous with psyche or psyche-soma and is being used to refer to a pathological defense organization.

Winnicott then asks what happens if the strain on the infant in response to "tantalizing early environment is greater and greater" (p. 246), exerting a pressure beyond the capacity of "mind" (in its pathological form) to handle. Under such strain, "One would expect confusional states, (and in the extreme) mental defect of the kind that is not dependent on brain-tissue deficiency" (p. 246). Under extreme strain, the infant's mental functioning is not able to process experience, which results in confusion and an inability to engage in the fundamentals of cognitive functioning ("mental defect"). Implicit is the idea that "erratic" (p. 246) or "tantalizing" (p. 246) mothering may be more difficult to handle than neglect.

When there are "lesser degrees" (p. 246) of tantalizing infant care, "we find *mental functioning becoming a thing in itself*" (p. 246, italics in original). Here, the reader must not only read Winnicott but also write Winnicott. To my mind, the phrase *"mental functioning becoming a thing in itself"* refers to a state I described earlier: mental functioning becoming a world of its own, a closed loop insulated from outside influence, and consequently isolated from experience of external objects from which to learn. In place of physical aliveness and the imaginative self is a hypertrophy of mental activity engaged in excessive thinking, figuring things out, and making sense of things. I would add that a tantalizing environment is forever promising, but never providing, to which the infant responds with delusions of omnipotence or autistic withdrawal, in which the infant is "practically replacing the good mother and making her unnecessary" (p. 246).

"Clinically, this can go along with dependence on the actual mother and a false personal growth on a compliance basis" (p. 246). In trying to understand what reliance on the "actual mother" means, I find I must write Winnicott here, too. In doing so, I rely on the concept of transitional phenomena (1951)—the space between fantasy and reality in which imagination (the imaginative self) lives—a concept Winnicott introduced two years after presenting the "Psyche-soma" paper to the British Psychological Society. Using the concept of transitional phenomena, I would say that the infant's dependence on "the actual mother" involves dependence on the real mother instead of dependence on a mother who is at once discovered and created or a mother with whom the infant comes alive. The infant relying on "the actual mother" persists (but is not alive) by responding "on a compliance basis" (p. 246), that is, by adapting to the mother's needs and wishes at the cost of genuine personal growth.

Under such circumstances,

> the psyche of the individual gets "seduced" away into this mind from the intimate relationship which the psyche originally had with the soma. The result is a mind-psyche, which is pathological.
>
> (p. 247)

In the face of maternal failure to adapt to the needs of the infant, which is experienced as a threat to continuity of being, the psyche is "seduced away" from psyche-soma and made part of a pathological organization that Winnicott calls *mind-psyche*. What is new here is the idea that mind-psyche includes psyche seduced away from psyche-soma. I would add that the seduction of psyche into mind-psyche saps the psyche of its capacity to imaginatively elaborate physical aliveness, which in turn diminishes the capacity of soma to form the core for the imaginative self. In this way, psyche and soma fall into a mutually depleting relationship.

Psyche is vulnerable to being "seduced away" from psyche-soma if forced into a defensive posture by threats to continuity of being and hence to fear of imminent annihilation. Psyche-soma seems to me to make a deal with the devil: the psyche is lured by the false promise of guaranteed survival at a time when it is faced by imminent annihilation. The infant defends himself by deadening himself and giving himself over, not to the tantalizing mother but to "the actual mother." The actual mother is no longer tantalizing because she is dead to the infant. He has rendered himself inert to her by dealing with her "on a compliance basis." The infant operating on the basis of a mind-psyche (as opposed to psyche-soma) is less tantalized and less threatened by imminent annihilation, all at the cost of the loss of aliveness and realness of self.

Winnicott then writes a paragraph in which he offers an example of the sort of person who functions with a mind-psyche. In such a person,

> one can observe a tendency for easy identification with the environmental aspect of all relationships that involve dependence... Clinically one may see such a person develop into one who is a *marvellously good mother to others* for a limited period; in fact a person who has developed along these lines may have almost magical *healing properties* because of an extreme capacity to make active adaptation to primitive needs.
> (p. 247, italics in original)

On first reading this passage, I thought that Winnicott is describing a relatively healthy person who is good at taking care of others. What could be wrong with this? Winnicott drops a hint: this person is able to perform these caretaking functions "for a limited period" (p. 247).

He continues his description of such a person with marvelously good healing skills:

> The falsity of these patterns for expression of the personality, however, becomes evident in practice. Breakdown threatens or occurs, because what the individual is all the time needing is *to find someone else* who will make real this "good environment" concept, so that the individual may return to the dependent psyche-soma which forms the only place to live from. In this case, "without mind" becomes a desired state.
> (p. 247, italics in original)

The quest of such an individual for someone to take care of him or her rings true, but it is not, for me, the most memorable part of the passage. The individual functioning with a mind isolated from psyche-soma is all the time needing to "return to the dependent psyche-soma which forms the only place to live from" (p. 247). The phrase "the only place to live from" defies paraphrase. What is it to "live from" the place of the dependent psyche-soma? Does "living from" mean "originating in" or "having one's roots in" or "being born of" or "coming to life in"? None of these, and all of these together and more, captures what one hears in the phrase "the only place to live from."

Winnicott adds, at the end of the paragraph: "In this case, 'without mind' becomes a desired state." This sort of person desires a somatic state free of mind in which psyche and soma, the alive body and the imaginative self, the soul, if you will, may be experienced. (*Psyche* is a word derived from the Indo-European word for "breathe" and for "soul," and seems particularly apt to describe Winnicott's conception of psyche-soma.)

The description Winnicott offers of the sort of person seeking a dependent place "to live from" reminds me of a patient of mine who, each year, cared for the children in her elementary school class with such devotion that she closed herself off almost entirely to the rest of the world. In the analysis, the patient looked after me. She would tell me that I should not meet with her on lesser national holidays because I "deserved a rest" and would say that I looked tired at times when I did feel tired, but no one else had noticed. The patient was a pleasant, but tedious, person to be with.

After some years of work, the patient had a dream: "I was at a pier unloading a ship. The work was very hard. As I hauled a large piece of furniture off the boat, I think it was a piano, I cut my hand badly, but I kept hauling the piece of furniture. I became weaker and weaker. I was on the ground on my back looking up at a group of people. I stared up at them expecting them to offer assistance, but they did nothing."

As I listened to the patient tell me the dream, I imagined her lying on her back on the couch looking up at me and finding me useless, which was a feeling I often had about myself when I was with her. I said, "You're all the people in the dream who are useless to you."

She was quiet, which was unusual for her. After a time, she said, "No, I'm the piano I try to carry around on my back."

I thought that the patient's interpretation was more useful than mine: what was useless to her was not a living person but a dead thing, a dead aspect of herself that she carried around. Nonetheless, what felt most significant about the patient's response was not her interpretation of the dream but her saying, "No," to me. She was refusing to cooperate. She was, in that moment, unwilling to take care of me by playing the appreciative patient, as was her wont. What felt most important to me lay in the patient's experience of saying, "No." In the context of all that had occurred in the analysis to that point, she was beginning to come to life as she transformed dead weight into alive refusal.

Clinical illustration

Winnicott then offers a clinical illustration of his "thesis" (p. 248). His thesis has expanded from the initial idea that the mind does not exist as an entity to an exploration of the nature of psyche and soma, of live body and imaginative self, as well as the functioning of a pathological mind-psyche. The clinical illustration further expands Winnicott's project in this paper to include a detailed analytic experience in which healthy psyche and soma emerge for the first time.

Winnicott's patient is a 47-year-old woman who "felt completely dissatisfied, as if always aiming to find herself and never succeeding" (p. 249). She was "generally liked; in fact I think she was never actively disliked" (p. 249): this is faint praise that communicates the way in which this patient was everybody's friend and a friend to nobody.

There was a period of this analysis in which the patient had a terrifying feeling that her head was being crushed. The patient came to experience this head-crushing not as something being done to her but as something she was doing to herself in order to rid herself of "false psyche" (p. 250) that did not feel as if it was a part of her. As time went on, "the word death became wrong [to refer to the head-crushing] and the patient began to substitute 'a giving in' and eventually the appropriate word was 'a not-knowing'" (p. 250). But the patient could not reach a full "acceptance of the not-knowing state" (p. 251).

Winnicott continues:

> At this point of not-knowing in this analysis there appeared a memory of a bird that was seen as "quite still except for the movements of the belly which indicated breathing."
>
> (p. 250)

During this period of the analysis, the patient repeatedly experienced a "gap in consciousness" (p. 251), "a blackout" with complete amnesia for the period of loss of consciousness. (It should be noted that a "gap in consciousness" is altogether different from a "gap in continuity of being." The former is a healthy development sought by Winnicott and his patient, while the latter is a threat to survival.) The patient had denied that gaps in consciousness had occurred throughout her life, but with her growing ability to accept a state of not knowing, the gap in consciousness "became something urgently sought" (p. 251). Such gaps were respites from the kind of excessive thinking (for example, her keeping a detailed diary of the entirety of her analysis) that had kept her unable to "find herself" (p. 249).

The patient became engaged in "violent head banging" (p. 251) in "an attempt to produce a blackout... an urgent need for the destruction of the mental processes located by the patient in her head" (p. 251). The patient was seeking a respite from this sort of thinking that "so easily becomes artificially a thing in itself" (p. 251). Again, I understand the state of becoming "artificially a thing in itself" to mean that the patient became ensnared in a closed loop of thinking that is isolated from all that is external to itself, which consequently renders her unable to learn or to grow. This state is "a thing in itself" in the sense that it is a world and a set of experiences unto itself cut off from everything and everyone external to the self.

It is important to pause here and imagine what Winnicott was dealing with clinically: a patient who was engaged in "violent head-banging." He does not say whether the head-banging occurred while the patient was with him or whether she did this somewhere else. In either case, it took restraint on his part, and confidence not only in the analytic process but in his own ability to differentiate head-banging as pathological self-destructiveness from head-banging as the healthiest part of the patient's personality, the part seeking a gap in excessive mental functioning that leaves her feeling unreal.

Winnicott then writes what I consider to be one of the most important passages in the paper and, for me, one of the most memorable clinical illustrations in his entire opus:

> The results of this bit of work [in which the patient was seeking a gap in consciousness] led to a temporary phase in which there was no mind and no mental functioning. There had to be a temporary phase in which the breathing of her body was all. In this way the patient became able to accept the not-knowing condition because I was holding her and keeping a continuity by my own breathing, while she let go, gave in, knew nothing; it could not be any good, however, if I held her and maintained my own continuity of life if she were dead. What made my part operative was that I could see and hear her belly moving as she breathed (like the bird) and therefore I knew that she was alive.
>
> (p. 252)

This movement in the session is mediated not by interpretation or any other spoken intervention. Winnicott says, "I was holding her and keeping a continuity by my own breathing." He was doing the work of psyche for both the patient and himself, while the patient "gave in, knew nothing." Winnicott communicates in the way he writes the beauty of "the music of breathing" by means of his use of softly recurring *b* sounds and long *e* sounds: "I could see and hear her belly moving as she breathed (like the bird)." And he ends the penultimate sentence of this passage with the word *dead* and ends the final sentence with the word *alive*. These are not effects a writer plans to create, but they are effects created in the act of writing when an author is writing well.

The "holding" that Winnicott is describing involves an intimate responsiveness of his own psyche-soma to that of the patient. "I was holding her and keeping a continuity by my own breathing." He was holding her in mind and holding her in body (in his own breathing). Holding is an ontological concept involving being and its relationship with time (here, continuity of breathing is the temporal element) (Ogden, 2004b). Though holding, in this instance, does not involve physical contact (as it does in the mother-infant relationship), it is at its core physically alive for both Winnicott and the patient.

But to leave it at what I have just said would be to miss a vitally important aspect of what was occurring in this session. The missing piece is much like the purloined letter—hidden in plain sight. I think that Winnicott was all the while bringing to the shared experience in which "the breathing of her body was all" the structure of the meaning in which the session was being lived. It seems to me that Winnicott came to the session under discussion with a general understanding of the patient's need to give up overactive mental functioning if she was to develop a living sense of self (alive psyche-soma). That structure of meaning was significantly elaborated as he spontaneously lived the experience with the patient. An aspect of Winnicott's work of knowing ("I knew that she was alive") included drawing moments of the past into the present: the patient's memory of the bird breathing, the head-banging, and the obsessional diary-writing. But his phrasing does more than bring past experience and past knowledge into the present. He is engaged in a particular type of remembering, what I would call remembering *parenthetically*: "(like the bird)."

Had someone else sat with this patient without bringing to the situation the structure of meaning Winnicott brought, the experience would not have been "any good" to her. What was critical was the combination of her experiencing of soma ("without mind") while Winnicott was experiencing and "witnessing" (Poland, 2000) the continuity of the patient's being/breathing "by my own breathing." "And therefore, I knew that she was alive." The structure of meaning that Winnicott brought to the session and developed in the session was communicated to the patient not in words but in the way he breathed, the way he moved in his chair, and so on.

Winnicott says that none of what happened could have occurred if the patient were dead. The patient was alive *because Winnicott had faith that she was alive*, and at the same time, the patient was alive *because she could feel and hear the movement of her own body breathing*. The two are not supplementary or complementary to one another; I would say that they are elements of a paradox that should not be solved.

Winnicott notes that something changed in the patient in the sessions following the one in which her breathing was all.

> Now for the first time she was able to have a psyche, an entity of her own, a body that breathes and in addition the beginning of fantasy belonging to the breathing and other physiological functions.
>
> (p. 252)

Winnicott is careful in his wording here. He says that the patient "was able to have a psyche, an entity of her own." He is using the word *entity* in a way that is different from the way he has been using it to this point in the paper. Here, *entity* does not refer to a localizable thing; rather it refers to the patient's experience of her own psyche-soma, which is now alive and real to her. It seems to me that the words "an entity of her own" may also refer to an identity of her own, a psyche of her own.

Then the phrase "a body that breathes" seems to me to refer to the patient's having not only a psyche (imaginative aliveness) that she feels to be her own but also a soma (physical aliveness) that also feels to be her own. This series of qualities of being alive concludes with "the beginning of fantasy belonging to the breathing." This is not a fantasy *about* breathing but a fantasy *belonging to* breathing that is imaginatively elaborated by psyche.

Perhaps Winnicott's knowing the patient was alive as he listened to her breathing-without-knowing-she-was-breathing is what could be called "perfect" adaptation: precisely what the patient needed without her having to know she needed it.

Winnicott goes on to say about the patient, "I suppose she would now be prepared to locate the psyche wherever the soma is alive" (p. 252). Winnicott does not say "wherever the body is alive." Winnicott plays with language here as he uses the terms "locate" and "wherever" to refer not to a place, as these words might seem to suggest, but to unlocalizable experiencing (pure verb, always in process) where psyche is alive in soma.

The concept of the unconscious mind in Winnicott's work

I would like to note something that lies at the heart not only of Winnicott's clinical illustration but of the paper as whole. What I am referring to is a shift Winnicott makes regarding the set of metaphors and concepts he relies on in his work as an analytic theorist and as a clinician. He is making use of a conception of mind different from the mind as described by Freud in his topographic model. The topographic model involves a conception of the conscious and unconscious mind separated by a repression barrier. Illness is the product of the demand for conscious expression (and the defenses against that expression) of repressed thoughts and feelings that are unacceptable. Winnicott would, I believe, strenuously reject the idea that his thinking in any way supplants or replaces the concept of the unconscious mind, for he would, I imagine, say that the concept of the unconscious is definitive of psychoanalysis. Nonetheless, it is telling that Winnicott uses the term *unconscious* only three times in his "Psyche-soma" paper.

Though I think that Winnicott views the topographic model as a vitally important set of concepts and metaphors, I also believe that he introduces a conception of analytic theory and practice in which a different set of concepts and metaphors occupy center stage. Winnicott is interested in a realm of experience in which questions regarding whether a thought or feeling or sensation or experience is conscious or unconscious simply does not arise. Instead, Winnicott understands the workings of psyche and soma in terms of aliveness and deadness, realness and unrealness, the live body and the imaginative self, being and disruption of continuity of being, as opposed to an understanding of the workings of psyche and soma in terms of the conscious and unconscious mind separated by a repression barrier.

From the perspective of the topographic model, let us look at the experiences with which Winnicott is concerned in this paper. Is physical aliveness a conscious or unconscious phenomenon? It makes no sense to even ask the question: the question does not apply. Aliveness has nothing to do with the repression barrier; it is an attribute of one's being. Being is neither a conscious nor an unconscious phenomenon. Nor do questions regarding the conscious and unconscious mind apply to the experience of imaginatively creating the experience of physical aliveness.

It is not easy to hold in mind the idea that there is a way of thinking analytically, a way of viewing the analytic process, that does not primarily rely on the concept of the conscious and unconscious mind. We must remind ourselves that the conscious and unconscious mind are only ideas, just as the ego and the id and the superego are ideas. Winnicott holds that there is no such "thing" as mind. By extension, there is no such "thing" as unconscious mind. We do not have two consciousnesses (conscious and unconscious), we have only one, which has qualities that are manifest and latent, and we make inferences about what is latent. What is implicit or latent content is called the unconscious in the topographic model, but it is only a model, a set of metaphors, which, like all metaphors, eventually grows stale.

Freud's topographic model is spatial in nature, conceiving of the conscious and unconscious mind as metaphorically "above and below" one another, separated by the repression barrier and a censorship function operating at the interface of the two. The topographic model is cast in terms of a play of psychic forces analogous to the play of force vectors in Newtonian physics. Winnicott's thinking is less spatial than Freud's, less focused on a play of psychic forces. Winnicott's thinking is more ontological (having to do with being and becoming), while Freud's topographic model is more epistemological (having to do with knowing and understanding and fear of knowing and understanding). I am pressing this point far beyond where Winnicott takes it.

We need not choose between the concepts and phenomena of aliveness and deadness, realness and unrealness, on the one hand, and the concepts of the conscious and unconscious mind, on the other. Winnicott's thinking is not *beyond* the topographic model, nor does it *supplant* the topographic model; it exists *alongside* the topographic model, and we make use of the set of ideas and metaphors that best helps us think at any given moment.

Concluding Comments

In "Mind and its relation to psyche-soma," Winnicott reinvents the concept of psyche-soma. For him, psyche refers to imaginatively elaborating somatic parts, feelings, and functions in a way that generates the experience of physical aliveness, and soma refers to the physical (not bodily) core of the imaginative self. The two are inseparable.

Soma is not to be confused with body, and psyche is not to be confused with brain. Both psyche and soma are unlocalizable, unfolding experiences.

Pathological mind, "mind-psyche," represents a seduction of psyche away from its intimate connection with soma into excessive mental functioning that feels dead and unreal to the individual.

Interestingly, Winnicott does not arrive at a definition of *mind* or its relation to psyche-soma. In "writing Winnicott," here, I take *mind* to mean higher or-der mental functioning including thinking, as opposed to more diffuse mental functioning, for example, the elaboration of consciousness itself. The latter would be a function of the broader category *psyche*.

In the face of failure of maternal adaptation beyond what the infant can tolerate, the infant relates to "the actual mother" "on a compliance basis." As I "write Winnicott," in healthy development of psyche, the infant relates to the creatively discovered mother who exists in a space between fantasy and reality.

In the clinical illustration, Winnicott reaches a point in the analytic work where the patient, who had been thoroughly in the grip of excessive men-tal functioning, experienced with Winnicott a state in which he took over the function of psyche while the patient experienced her own breathing in a state of almost pure somatic aliveness. In my view, Winnicott enters this experience with a structure of meaning he has accrued in the course of the analysis, without which the experience with the patient would not have been "operative."

Winnicott in this paper and throughout his opus elaborates an understand-ing of analytic theory and practice in which the qualities of experience that are held to be most important include aliveness and deadness, realness and unrealness, continuity of being and disruption of continuity of being. These qualities of life do not lend themselves to being divided along the lines of conscious and unconscious mind (the topographic model). I view the trans-formations of experience addressed by Winnicott as constituting a form of analytic thinking that exists alongside of, not as a replacement for, transforma-tions of experience addressed by the topographic model. The analyst makes use of the set of terms that best helps him or her to think at any given juncture.

References

Ogden, T. H. (2004a). Dreaming undreamt dreams and interrupted cries. *Int. J. Psychoanal. 85*: 855–857.

Ogden, T. H. (2004b). On holding and containing, being and dreaming. *Int. J. Psychoanal.* 85: 1349–1364.

Ogden, T. H. (2019). Ontological psychoanalysis or "What do you want to be when you grow up?" *Psychoanal. Q.* 88: 661–6954

Poland, W. (2000). The analyst's witnessing and otherness. *J. Am. Psychoanal. Assn.* 48: 80–93.

Scott, W. C. M. (1949). The body scheme in psychotherapy. *Brit. J. Med. Psychol.* 22.

Winnicott, D. W. (1947). Hate in the countertransference. In *Through Paediatrics to Psycho-Analysis*. New York: Basic Books, pp. 194–203.

Winnicott, D. W. (1949). Mind and its relation to the psyche-soma. In *Through Paediatrics to Psycho-Analysis*. New York: Basic Books, pp. 243–254.

Winnicott, D. W. (1951). Transitional objects and transitional phenomena. In *Playing and Reality*. New York: Basic Books, 1971, pp. 1–25.

Winnicott, D. W. (1952). Psychoses and child care. In *Through Paediatrics to Psycho-Analysis*. New York: Basic Books, pp. 219–228.

Winnicott, D. W. (1958). The capacity to be alone. In *The Maturational Processes and the Facilitating Environment*. New York: International Universities Press, pp. 29–36.

Winnicott, D. W. (1960). The theory of the parent-infant relationship. *Int. J. Psychoanal.* 41: 585–595.

7   Transformations at the dawn of verbal language

The transformation that occurs at the advent of verbally symbolic language constitutes a major turning point both in terms of what one is able to experience and in terms of the nature of one's subjectivity, of one's sense of I-ness, and of who one feels oneself to be.

The acquisition of verbally symbolic language underlies the creation of a subjectivity with which one does not simply experience *what is*, but also has ideas *about* what is happening and *about who one is*.[1] In dreaming, we are dealing with nonverbal, imagistic presentations of what is. Before one has acquired verbal symbolization, one can take no distance on the experience of the dream. The dream is what it is. There is no "I" observing "me" in the experience; there is no thinking about one's thinking; there is no self-reflection; all there is is what is.

Hallucinatory, paranoid, and manic ideation are preverbal in nature. Such thoughts are experienced as *perceptions of* something, not as *thoughts about* something. One cannot think about one's hallucinatory, paranoid, or manic ideation; one can only elaborate it.

In what follows, I will flesh out the nature of preverbal experience, the transformations that occur with the birth of verbally symbolic language, and the nature of experience once verbally symbolic language has been achieved.

Signs and symbols

I will be using the term *sign* to refer to a communication in which there is a direct relationship between an element of expression (a sign) and what it refers to (a content). For instance, the shape of horseshoes in the snow is a sign indicating that a horse or horses have been there.

By contrast, a symbol does not bear a direct relationship to what it names or refers to. For instance, the word *bird* or the letters b-i-r-d (symbols) bear no relationship to the animal they name (the symbolized). The preverbal symbolization of infants is based on signs (direct relationship to what is referred to); for example, the baby's shriek indicates that she is in pain and her throwing food to the floor indicates the displeasure or frustration she is feeling.

DOI: 10.4324/9781003528821-8

Freud (1900, 1915) envisioned the system preconscious as the part of the topographic model of the mind that transforms preverbal symbolization (for example, unconscious ideation and the visual imagery of dreaming) into verbally symbolic language that is used in conscious, secondary process thinking. Conscious thinking is based on the cause-and-effect logic in diachronic (sequential) time. Ever-present in the psyche, as Freud envisioned it, is pressure from the preverbal, repressed unconscious to enter the conscious domain in such forms as forgetting, confusion, symptom formation, humor, and the background colorations and intensities the unconscious lends to consciousness. The use of verbally symbolic language and conscious secondary process thinking are seen by Freud as yielding the capacity for self-reflection which forms the basis for a therapeutic analytic process that occurs within the individual and within the analytic setting.

Segal (1957) offers a psychoanalytic perspective on the relationship between what she calls "symbolic equation" (p. 395) and "symbol formation proper" (p. 395). These forms of symbolization are roughly equivalent to the linguistic categories of symbolization in the forms of signs and symbols, respectively. Symbolic equation is preverbal and associated with the paranoid-schizoid position (in which one relates to primitive part objects), while the latter, symbol formation proper, is associated with the depressive position (in which one relates maturely to whole objects). Segal posits that in a state of mind in which symbolic equation is dominant, the experience of playing the violin may be equated with masturbating, so the individual would not play the violin in public. By contrast, when symbol formation proper is dominant (in the depressive position), the symbol (for instance, playing the violin) may serve as a representation of an unconscious sexual phantasy concerning masturbation, but the phantasy is not experienced as identical to the act of playing the violin. Their relationship is symbolic.

For Winnicott, the infant at the start lives in a state of "going on being" (Winnicott, 1949, p. 245). The phrase *going on being* (a phrase without a subject) designates a state in which the infant has not yet achieved a sense of I-ness interacting with otherness. In a state of going on being, subjectivity (a sense of I-ness) is held for the infant by the mother. For Winnicott (1968), preverbal forms of communication between mother and infant and patient and analyst are at times more expressive than verbally symbolic communication:

> A patient dug her nails into the skin of my hand at a moment of intense feeling. My interpretation was "Ow!" This scarcely involved my intellectual equipment at all, and it was quite useful because it came *immediately,* (not after a pause for reflection) and because it meant to the patient that my hand was alive, that it was part of me, and that I was there to be used.
>
> (Winnicott, 1968, p. 95)

Here, Winnicott illustrates the way in which preverbal communication ("Ow") carries meaning ("my hand was alive, that it was part of me") more effectively than could be done in verbally symbolized communication (derived from self-reflection). This forms the basis for Winnicott's cautioning analysts to restrain themselves from offering interpretations (verbal symbolizations of and understanding of the patient's experience) and instead to allow the patient the joy of the *experience* of discovering meaning on his or her own (1969, p. 86).

Before verbally symbolic language is established, mother and infant communicate in what Grotstein calls "baby talk" (Grotstein, 2015, personal communication), a language in which needs, affection, frustration, and much else are communicated in the form of a multitude of signs: a dreamy look in one's eyes, the molding of bodies, a quality of sucking at the breast and of cries in the night, and "a thousand ways that compare with the infinite variety of poetry" (Winnicott, 1968, p. 95). And it is difficult not to hear in this preverbal communication the first experience of music. (See Litowitz [2011] for a discussion of preverbal communication in the mother-infant relationship and in the relationship between patient and analyst.)

The domain of verbally symbolic thought

With the development of verbally symbolic thought a new world of experience opens to us.[2] We can create symbols not only for objects (names such as tree, car, and airplane) but also for feeling states (jealousy, guilt, compassion), as well as for abstract ideas (time, death, the solar system). Having names for things, feelings, and ideas changes everything.

With the development of the capacity for verbal language, a more complex subjectivity is generated. In this subjectivity, the subject, in the process of verbally symbolizing, occupies the "space" between the symbol and the symbolized. The individual becomes the interlocutor of his own experience, the person in charge of using the vast set of words (verbal symbols) to construct meaning that defines himself and the world. With the achievement of verbal language, "I" as subject and "me" as object are created in the same moment. There can be no object (me) without an "I" to observe it, and there can be no "I" without otherness (me as object). Otherness takes the form of me-as-object and the form of everything that is not-me.[3]

With verbal language, one is not only able to communicate with others in words, but one also thinks in words. One becomes able to think about oneself and about one's thinking. A world is created in which things do not simply happen; instead, things happen to an observing self whose perceptual apparatus is his and his alone. Each individual is the interpreting center of his own universe. Everything that happens is not simply happening (as in dreaming and other forms of preverbal experience); things are happening to a subject capable not only of perception but of apperception (understanding what is happening by integrating experience into a set of ideas one already has). I, a self-reflective entity, am experiencing what is happening and trying to make sense of it.

A doll, for a preverbal infant or small child, is an entity into which she has projected an aspect of her internal world. For the infant or child, the doll becomes a container or personification of the infant's or child's internal state. The doll may be happy or sad, awake or asleep, hungry or full, and in any other state the child has experienced. The feelings and movements of the doll bear a direct relationship with what the child attributes to it. There is no interpreting subject mediating between the doll and the states being attributed to it. What you see is what you get—a doll happily dancing is a living figure, much like the child feeling happy.

Verbally symbolic language, by contrast, not only names experience, it creates the possibility of experiencing one's life in a qualitatively different way. Not only do a far broader set of emotions become possible, subjectivity itself is qualitatively altered. One is able to have such experiences as reflecting on a choice one has made, regretting what one has said, not knowing why that never came to mind, seeing the connection between the manifest and the latent aspects of oneself or someone else. The new subjectivity involves a complex relationship between oneself as subject (I) and oneself as object (me). One experiences an ever-shifting relationship (often a disjunction) between one's sense of who one is and the actual way one thinks, feels, and behaves. Such experiences cannot occur to the preverbal infant or child. The mother adjusts to the infant's psychic state of mind in which subject and object, I and me, are not yet clearly differentiated by speaking to the infant with language that does not differentiate between subject and object. She speaks as if she is an object (not a subject) by referring to herself in the third person: "Mommy is happy" or "Mommy is leaving."

Before the development of verbally symbolic language, the infant is able to perceive a dog, but there is not yet the idea of a dog, which involves not only a conception of a dog but also a conception of oneself thinking of a dog. To create the idea of a dog, there must be a subject mediating between the perceived dog and the general category of dogs. In a preverbal era of experience, the family dog is the family dog, not a subset of the concept of animals and living things and dead things. For the preverbal infant, seeing his mother crying can be experienced only in terms of the range of feelings the infant is able to experience; the experience of the mother crying cannot be thought about; it can only be reacted to.

In verbally symbolic thought, one is able to experience feelings of compassion, sadness, despair, guilt, melancholia, and mournful loss. The infant is able to respond to experience on a visceral level but cannot create affective response with the nuance of verbally symbolic language. The nature of experience in a preverbal world involves a visceral flow along dimensions, more or less, of good or bad, safe or dangerous, hungry or sated, happy or sad.

The creation of meaning

The psychic changes that occur as the individual acquires verbally symbolic language are addressed with particular lucidity by two Brazilian analysts

(Rocha Barros, 2000, 2018; Rocha Barros and Rocha Barros, 2018). They build upon Cassirer's (1944) and Langer's (1942) works on the philosophy of language:

> In the act of interpreting [a dream]... we transmute one symbolic basis—in this case the language expressive of the visually symbolic experience of the dream or reverie—into another symbolic basis, that of verbally symbolic interpretation... *Meaning is not only named by interpretation of dreams and reveries, it is created* in the transmutation from one symbolic basis to another.
>
> (Rocha Barros, 2018, p. 228, italics added)

Rocha Barros is referring here to the process in which the individual on waking begins to understand (interpret) his own dreams by transforming them into verbally symbolic form. With the capacity for verbal language, the individual, on awaking from a dream, is able to talk with himself or herself or with someone else *about* the dream. For a psychotic patient, a dream is what it is; it is indecipherable from a hallucination. For a nonpsychotic patient, a dream while being dreamt is what it is. It is a preverbal imagistic experience. But on waking, when the dreamer is capable of verbally symbolic thoughts, the dream is a symbolic communication between different aspects of oneself.

Grotstein (1979) and Sandler (1976) have proposed that unconscious understanding of dreams and consequent psychic growth occur by means of communication between different aspects of the unconscious mind. Verbally symbolic thought or something akin to it occurs in communication between what Grotstein (1979) calls "the [unconscious] dreamer who dreams the dream" and "the [unconscious] dreamer who understands the dream" (p. 110) and what Sandler (1976) calls the unconscious "dream-work" and "understanding-work" (p. 40). These contributions account for the value to the individual, in terms of potential contribution to psychic growth, of all the dreams one dreams but is unable to remember.

The capacity for verbally symbolizing one's experience (including the dreams one remembers) creates a sea change in the experience of oneself in relation to one's dreaming. Not only is the meaning of the dream created when transformed into verbally symbolic form, the experience of oneself in relation to the dream is newly created. What had been an experience in which what you see is what you get becomes an experience in which an I-me dialectic is established: dreaming becomes differentiated into "me" (the dream as object to be understood) in relation to the interpreting subject ("I") who is doing the work of understanding. (See Hook [2002] for a discussion of the I-me dialectic as constructed in the process of speech.)

When speaking of the experience of acquiring verbally symbolic language, it is important to distinguish between *the meaning that is created,* on the one hand, and *the experience of creating meaning,* on the other. These two aspects of experiencing are inseparable. The *meaning that is created* holds significance in what I call the epistemological dimension of psychoanalysis, the dimension having to do with coming to understand oneself and the world in which one lives. In contrast, the *experience of creating meaning* is an aspect of what I call the ontological dimension of the analytic process, the dimension having to do with being and becoming more fully oneself (Ogden, 2019, 2021, 2024). When an analyst offers an interpretation of a dream, the patient may find the experience valuable in arriving at an *understanding* of an aspect of himself from which he has felt disconnected and lifeless. For another patient, that same interpretation may be significant not as an enhancement of self-understanding but as an *experience of being recognized and understood* for who she is. The *meaning created* is verbally symbolized; the *experience of creating meaning* is predominantly preverbal. The two—the *meaning created* and the *experience of creating meaning*—are inseparable aspects of the therapeutic value of analytic experience.

In the analytic situation, I conceive of the analytic third (1994) as an unconscious third subjectivity co-created by patient and analyst. This subjectivity is, like dreaming, predominantly a preverbal form of creating meaning, as opposed to a process focused on making use of the meanings created in the course of verbal symbolization.

Pathological forms of the analytic third ("the subjugating third" [Ogden, 1996, p. 1123]) are also experiences of creating meaning, though these experiences are self-destructive in the sense that the meaning being created is that of the destruction of meaning. For instance, in the case of a perverse intersubjectivity, the subject and object are engaged in destroying the experience of psychic deadness by means of the experience of feeling sexually excited in a way that feels utterly empty (Ogden, 1996).

The marvel of it

The transformation that occurs with the achievement of verbally symbolic language is, to my mind, nowhere better described than by Helen Keller (1903).

> One day, while I was playing with my new doll, Miss Sullivan put my big rag doll into my lap and also spelled "d-o-l-l" and tried to make me understand that "d-o-l-l" applied to both. [Miss Sullivan drew with her finger the shapes of the letters d-o-l-l on the palm of 7-year-old Helen's hand.] Earlier in the day we had had a tussle over the words "m-u-g" and "w-a-t-e-r." Miss Sullivan had tried to impress it upon me that "m-u-g" is *mug* and that "w-a-t-e-r" is *water*, but I persisted in confounding the two. In despair she had dropped the subject for the time, only to renew it at the first opportunity. I became impatient at her repeated attempts and, seizing the new doll, I dashed it upon the floor. I was keenly delighted when I felt the fragments of the broken doll at my feet. Neither sorrow nor regret followed my passionate outburst. I had not loved the doll. In the still, dark world in which I lived there was no strong sentiment or tenderness.
>
> (pp. 11–12)

Here, Keller describes her dashing the doll as a sign of her frustration concerning understanding what her teacher, Anne Sullivan, was trying to teach her. She was unable to feel a wide range of emotions, in particular, feelings of sorrow, regret, love, and tenderness. Helen was confined primarily to a preverbal world of signs in which the sign bore a direct relationship to the signified. Her throwing the doll to the floor (the sign) bore a direct correspondence with the signified (her feeling angry and frustrated).

When her teacher (thus far without a name for Helen) swept up the pieces of the broken doll,

> I had a sense of satisfaction that my source of discomfort was removed. She brought me my hat and I knew we were going out into the warm sunshine. This thought, if a wordless sensation can be called a thought, made me hop and skip with pleasure.
>
> (p. 12)

Here, Keller distinguishes between having a thought and having "a wordless sensation."

Keller goes on to describe the change she experienced on achieving the capacity for verbally symbolic language which occurred upon recognizing the connection between the word *water* and water itself:

> I left the well-house eager to learn. Everything had a name, and each name gave birth to a new thought. As we returned to the house every object which I touched seemed to quiver with life. That was because I saw everything with the strange, new sight that had come to me. On entering the door I remembered the doll I had broken. I felt my way to the hearth and picked up the pieces. I tried vainly to put them together. Then my eyes filled with tears; for I realized what I had done, and for the first time I felt repentance and sorrow.
>
> (p. 12)

Keller goes on to describe subsequent events of that day.

> I learned a great many new words that day. I do not remember what they all were, but I do know that mother, father, sister, teacher were among them—words that were to make the world blossom for me.
>
> (p. 12)

With the acquisition of verbally symbolic language, there developed a new way of experiencing, a new way of coming into being, and a new way of being alive. Emotions that she had not previously been able to feel—repentance and sorrow and love—Helen became able to experience. It is not that these feelings were latent and were waiting to be unearthed. This is emphatically not the case. These feelings were created for the first time when Keller entered the world of experience verbally symbolized. "Everything had a name, and each name gave birth to a new thought... every object which I touched seemed to quiver with life." Names are not simply *designations* for feelings and things, they are *ideas* about feelings and people and things. Language gives rise to a qualitatively different realm of experience, a realm in which one is both subject and object, one is able to think of oneself thinking, one is alive to levels of meaning, range of emotion, complexity of feeling, and forms of experiencing not previously attainable.

Concluding comment

Preverbal language, which involves a direct relationship between sign and signified, is based in early development on binary opposites. This can be a powerful form of communication between mother and infant ("baby talk") and analyst and patient "with the infinite variety of poetry." Much in the mother-infant relationship and the analytic relationship can only be communicated in this symbolic form.

With the acquisition of verbally symbolic language, we are not simply understanding something more about our experience, we are creating a new form of experiencing, we are experiencing differently, and consequently coming into being in a different way. As the I-me dialectic comes into being, self-reflection becomes possible. One becomes able to experience a far broader range and depth of emotion in relation to others who are experienced as whole and separate people. There is the joy of communicating in words with oneself and with others, which opens up a world that "quivers with life."

Notes

1 Basch (1983) anticipated some of these ideas in his treatise on the progression from automatic "affective" responses in infancy to the reflective emotional life that becomes increasingly possible with the development of verbal language.
2 It should be borne in mind that preverbal is not synonymous with nonverbal. The communication between mother and infant reflects from the outset the development of language structures that will eventually become full verbally symbolized speech (Vivona, 2012).
3 See Ricoeur (1992).

References

Basch, M. F. (1976). The concept of affect: A re-examination. *Int. J. Psychoanal.* 24: 759–777.
Cassirer, E. (1944). *An Essay on Man: An Introduction to a Philosophy of Human Culture.* New Haven, CT: Yale University Press.
Freud, S. (1900). The Interpretation of Dreams. *S.E.* 4/5. London: Hogarth Press, 1955.
Freud, S. (1915). The unconscious. *S.E.* 14. London: Hogarth Press, 1955.
Grotstein, J. (1979). Who is the dreamer who dreams the dream and who is the dreamer who understands it—A psychoanalytic inquiry into the ultimate nature of being. *Contemp. Psychoanal.* 15: 110–169.

Hook, D. (2002). The other side of language: The body and the limits of signification. *Psychoanal. Rev.* 86: 681–713.

Keller, H. (1903). *The Story of My Life*. Mineola, NY: Dover Publications, 1996.

Langer, S. K. (1942). *Philosophy in a New Key: A Study in the Symbolism of Reason, Rite and Art*. Cambridge, MA: Harvard University Press.

Litowitz, B. (2011). From dyad to dialogue: Language and the early relationship in American psychoanalytic theory. *J. Am. Psychoanal. Assn.* 59: 483–507.

Ogden, T.H. (1994). The analytic third: Working with intersubjective clinical facts. *Int. J. Psychoanal.* 75: 3–20.

Ogden, T. H. (1996). The perverse subject of analysis. *J. Amer. Psychoanal. Assn.* 77: 883–889.

Ogden, T. H. (2019). Ontological psychoanalysis, or what do you want to be when you grow up? *Psychoanal. Q.* 88: 13–21.

Ogden, T. H. (2020). Toward a revised form of analytic theory and practice: The evolution of analytic theory of mind. *Psychoanal. Q.* 89: 219–243.

Ogden, T. H. (2024). Ontological psychoanalysis in clinical practice. *Psychoanal. Q.* 93: 13–31.

Ricoeur, P. (1995). *Oneself as Another*. Chicago, IL: University of Chicago Press.

Rocha Barros, E. M. (2000). Affect and pictographic image: The constitution of meaning. *Int. J. Psychoanal.* 81: 1087–1089.

Rocha Barros, E. M. (2018). Symbol formation and transformation in theory and in practice. *Canadian J. Psychoanal.* 26: 222–237.

Rocha Barros, E. M. & Rocha Barros, E. L. (2018). Klein yesterday, today and tomorrow: Reflections on her 1936 lecture on technique. *Int. J. Psychoanal.* 99: 968–978.

Sandler, J. (1976). Dreams, unconscious fantasies, and "identity of perception." *Int. Rev. Psychoanal.* 3: 33–42.

Segal, H. (1957). Notes on symbol formation. *Int. J. Psychoanal.* 38: 391–387.

Vivona, J. (2012). Is there a nonverbal period of development? *J. Amer. Psychoanal. Assn.* 60: 231–265.

Winnicott, (1949). Mind and its relation to psyche-soma. In *Through Paediatrics to Psycho-Analysis*. New York: Basic Books, 1958, pp. 229–244.

Winnicott, D. W. (1968). Communication between infant and mother, mother and infant compared. In *What Is Psychoanalysis?* ed. W. Joffe. London: Balliere, Tindall, and Cassell, pp. 89–103.

Winnicott, D. W. (1969). The use of an object and relating through identifications. In *Playing and Reality*. New York: Basic Books, 1971, pp. 86–94.

8   Discovering a personal life

On Winnicott's "The capacity to be alone"

Many, if not most, of Winnicott's most important contributions to psycho-analysis—for example, the concepts of transitional objects and phenomena, the experience of playing, creative experience of every sort, the feeling of real, what alive means, the incommunicado core self, the capacity to be alone, potential space, the use of an object, and a third area of experiencing that lies outside of the realm of the internal world and the external world—all involve paradoxical thinking. This form of thinking is perhaps Winnicott's most important contribution to psychoanalysis.

Winnicott's 1958 paper "The capacity to be alone" holds an important place in the development of his paradoxical thinking.[1] That paper contains Winnicott's first use of the term *paradox* in his published work. Even in "Transitional objects and transitional phenomena" (1953), where Winnicott first makes use of paradoxical thinking, he does not use the term *paradox*. Only in the expanded version of the original "Transitional object" paper, which he published 18 years later (Winnicott, 1971a), does Winnicott add the term *paradox* to his discussion of transitional objects and phenomena.

"The capacity to be alone" is a study in paradoxical thinking. To my mind, if one is to understand this paper, one must think paradoxically while reading virtually every sentence of it. This makes the paper a very difficult paper.

Winnicott begins the paper: "I wish to make an examination of the capac-ity of the individual to be alone, acting on the assumption that this capacity is one of the most important signs of maturity in emotional development" (1958, p. 29). Winnicott then adds that there is much more written in the ana-lytic literature "on the *fear* of being alone or the *wish* to be alone than on the *ability* to be alone" (p. 29, italics in original). He concludes that "a discussion on the *positive* aspects of the capacity to be alone is overdue" (p. 29, italics in original).

Three- and two-body relationships

Winnicott attempts to locate the capacity to be alone in relation to three- and two-body relationships. The Oedipus complex is a stage dominated by a three-body relationship. Klein's concept of the depressive position is

DOI: 10.4324/9781003528821-9

illustrative of a two-body relationship between mother and infant who have achieved differentiation from one another. Winnicott says that it would be natural to think of narcissism as an example of a one-body relationship, but "I am suggesting that this jump from two-body relationships to a one-body relationship cannot, in fact, be made without violation of a great deal that we know through our analytic work and through direct observation of mothers and infants" (p. 30). To my mind, Winnicott's dismissal of a one-body relationship is his way of insisting that the infant is never alone, and this idea paves the way for his paradoxical conception of the capacity to be alone.

Paradox

Winnicott states in the space of two sentences what he believes to be the principal idea of the paper:

> The main point of this contribution can now be stated. Although many types of experience go to the establishment of the capacity to be alone, there is one that is basic, and without a sufficiency of it the capacity to be alone does not come about; *this experience is that of being alone, as an infant and small child, in the presence of mother.* Thus the basis of the capacity to be alone is a paradox; it is the experience of being alone while someone else is present.
>
> (p. 30, italics in original)

The capacity to be alone is paradoxical: the individual is alone *and* in the presence of someone else. This paradox is not to be resolved, for example, by saying that the infant is alone but not alone because the mother is present as an internal object. To resolve the paradox in this way is to miss the point of Winnicott's paper. From the perspective of paradox, the infant is alone *and* the infant is in the presence of the mother. Both are true, and neither supplants the veracity of the other. It is very difficult for me to hold this paradox in mind without slipping into a resolution of it. Winnicott, in the introduction to *Playing and Reality* (1971b), asks the reader to grant him this request:

> My contribution is to ask for a paradox to be accepted and tolerated and respected, and for it not to be resolved. By flight to split-off intellectual functioning it is possible to resolve the paradox, but the price of this is the loss of the value of the paradox itself.
>
> (p. xii)

Winnicott elaborates his conception of the paradox involved in the capacity to be alone:

> Here is implied a rather special type of relationship, that between the infant or small child who is alone, and the mother or mother-substitute

who is in fact reliably present even if represented for the moment by a cot or a pram or the general atmosphere of the immediate environment.

(p. 30)

In this statement of the paradox, there is a *relationship* between the infant who is alone and the mother who is present (or present in the form of a representation of her as an external object). The mother is "in fact reliably present," and she is at the same time absent.

Why is it important to bear in mind that the mother (who is present) is not part of an internal object relationship, and instead is present or symbolically present in bits of the external world (in the form of a pram or the environment in general)? To my mind, this distinction is crucial because the capacity to be alone involves a relationship with the external object world, not a relationship with oneself or one's internal object world. The mother who is present when the infant is alone is a fully differentiated external object.

This paradox is closely related to the paradox underlying the relationship with transitional objects and phenomena which are at once created and discovered. The doll a little girl is playing with is (paradoxically) a real baby *and* a make-believe baby. To ask her if the doll is real or make-believe would be to disrupt her experience of playing. The real and the make-believe are coexistent elements of the paradox underlying the experience of playing (and every other creative activity).

Ego-relatedness

Winnicott now tells us, "Personally I like to use the term ego-relatedness [in connection with the capacity to be alone], which is convenient in that it contrasts rather clearly with the word id-relationship, which is a recurring complication in what might be called ego life" (pp. 30–31).

I am always taken by surprise when Winnicott adopts the terms of Freud's structural model—id, ego, and superego—to express his own ideas. Winnicott's own thinking adds a new dimension to the structural model's metaphor of the "committee" composed of bodily impulse (id), moral judgment and idealization (superego), and efforts to balance and integrate conflicting internal demands with external reality (ego). Winnicott shifts the focus of analytic inquiry from a study of the interplay of id, ego, superego, and external reality to an inquiry into the ways one comes into being with a feeling that one is whole, alive, real, imaginative, and personal. The ways one comes into being in these ways are inexpressible in the terms of the structural model. Winnicott's focus is on the ever-unfolding experience of coming into being, which is fundamentally an experience of the paradoxical interplay of subjectivity and objectivity.

Winnicott also creates new analytic language that supplements the language of Freud's topographic model in which the mind is viewed as having conscious, preconscious, and unconscious components. (The structural model presupposes the terms of the topographic model.) Winnicott does not reject the topographic model of the mind; he adds paradoxical concepts to the linear, sequential, cause-and-effect thinking underlying that model. It makes no sense to ask if being alone, in the sense Winnicott is conceiving of it, is a conscious or an unconscious phenomenon. It exists on a different conceptual plane.

With these aspects of Winnicott's contribution in mind, one might ask why he uses the terms "ego-relatedness" and "id-relatedness" in this paper. I do not have an answer to this question, but I imagine that it was important to Winnicott not to be accused of not being a "Freudian," not being a "real" psychoanalyst. Melanie Klein had been accused of not being a Freudian, and instead being a "Kleinian" (a term said to be coined by Anna Freud during the Controversial Discussions). It seems to me that Klein may have attempted to maintain her credentials as a "Freudian" by using Freud's term *death instinct* to refer to her own entirely different conception of the death instinct. Winnicott may be doing something similar here (whether or not he is aware of it) when he uses the terms *ego* and *id* instead of using his own language of self and desire, but this is mere speculation on my part.

In reading Winnicott's discussion of "ego-relatedness," the reader must not only read Winnicott but also write Winnicott. He says, "Ego-relatedness refers to the relationship between two people, one of whom at any rate is alone; perhaps both are alone, yet the presence of each is important to the other" (p. 31). In ego-relatedness, one or both people are alone, that is, capable of living in the (paradoxical) psychic state in which one is alone while being in the presence of another person. In that state, one is alive and real to oneself and in one's relatedness to the other. Under such circumstances, Winnicott says the word "like" better refers to ego-relatedness and "loving is more a matter of id-relationships, either crude or in sublimated form" (p. 31). It seems to me implicit that the feeling of love has a greater component of sexual desire than does friendship, but friendship involves its own unique form of closeness.

Winnicott gives us a clue concerning his use of the terms "ego" and "id": "I wish to remind you how it would be possible to refer to the capacity to be alone in well-worn psycho-analytic phraseology" (p. 31). The use of the term "well-worn" suggests, but only suggests, that he views the contributions of Freud and Klein, which he is about to discuss, as tired and ill-equipped to deal with the phenomena involved in the capacity to be alone.

Winnicott says that Freud conceives of being alone as similar to the time "after satisfactory intercourse" (p. 31) when one is alone with "another person who is also alone" (p. 31). Such solitude is "relatively free from the property that we call 'withdrawal'" (p. 31). Freud also conceives of the infant's capacity to be alone as the outcome of the child's acceptance of the primal scene in the form of masturbation in which

the whole responsibility for the conscious and unconscious fantasy is accepted by the individual child, who is the third person in a three-body or triangular relationship. To be able to be alone in these circumstances implies a maturity of erotic development... and it implies a tolerance of ambivalence.

(p. 31)

Freud's way of thinking is quite linear and clearly has little to do with Winnicott's conception of the capacity to be alone.

Winnicott then presents Klein's theory of the capacity to be alone which

depends on the existence of a good object in the psychic reality of the individual. The good internal breast or penis or the good internal relationships are well enough set up and defended for the individual... to feel confident about the present and the future. The relationship of the individual to his or her internal objects... provides of itself a sufficiency of living, so that temporarily he or she is able to rest contented even in the absence of external objects and stimuli.

(p. 32)

So, from Winnicott's perspective, Klein provides an object-relations theory of the capacity to be alone. The establishment of an internal object relationship with the mother, from Klein's perspective, makes it possible for the infant or child to be alone while feeling "confident about the present and the future," that is, while feeling safe. As I mentioned earlier, an understanding of the mother's presence (in the experience of being alone) as taking the form of an internal object relationship collapses the paradox Winnicott is presenting.

Even as Winnicott addresses the ideas of Freud and Klein, he seems unable to resist amplifying the power of their ideas by substituting bits of his own language for those of Freud and Klein. For instance, in discussing Klein, Winnicott uses the term "sufficiency of living" (p. 32), a phrase never used by Klein, to describe the internal world she envisions.

To be alone in an immature state

Winnicott insists that while the capacity to be alone is a mark of the maturity and sophistication of the individual, this capacity has its roots in an immature form of infantile experience.

Being alone in the presence of someone can take place at a very early stage, when the *ego immaturity is naturally balanced by ego-support* from the mother.

(p. 32, italics in original)

The sentence that follows adds a complication: "In the course of time the individual introjects the ego-supportive mother and in this way becomes able to be alone without frequent reference to the mother or mother symbol" (p. 32). I am at first confused by the term *introjects* because the idea of an introjected mother collapses the paradox underlying the capacity to be alone. What Winnicott may be referring to when he uses the term *introjects* is the achievement of a mature psychic state in which the individual develops an aspect of self that provides the supportive *function* the mother once provided without becoming an internal object representation of the mother. The infant becomes able to create a sense of the mother as external object without her having to play that role. In this way, the individual becomes able, on his or her own, to do the psychic work of creating the paradoxical psychic state of being alone in the presence of someone external to himself or herself.

I am reminded here of a diagram Winnicott draws in "Psychoses and child care" (1952) in which there is an outer circle representing the mother and a circle within that circle representing the infant. The infant rests in a state of healthy isolation within the environment of the mother who is present as unobtrusively as water is for a fish. The mother (the outer circle) is present, but invisible to the infant unless the infant becomes interested in her, either out of curiosity or out of need, in which case he seeks her out (bends the inner circle toward the outer one). If the mother seeks the infant (bends inward to touch the inner circle) before the infant is ready for her to become visible as an external object, the mother's gesture constitutes an impingement upon the infant and demands defensive compliance from him. So, too, in the experience of being alone, if the mother makes her presence known in an unwanted or unneeded way, the paradoxical experience of being alone collapses.

I am alone

Winnicott plays with the sentence "I am alone." The word "I," he says, conveys the idea that "the individual is established as a unit" (p. 33). The words "I am" convey the idea that "the individual not only has shape but also life" (p. 33). And the words "I am alone" suggest that in addition to the infant being a unit and having life, "there is an appreciation on the part of the infant of the mother's continued existence" (p. 33). There is an "appreciation" by the infant of the mother's continued existence despite the fact that he is alone. I find the word *appreciation* to be a word that is just right to convey Winnicott's sense of the infant's experience of the external object mother while he or she is alone.

Ego-relatedness as the matrix of transference

Winnicott, at this point, further develops his concept of ego-relatedness.

> Now, if I am right in the matter of this paradox [involved in the capacity to be alone], it is interesting to examine the nature of the relationship of the infant to the mother, that which for the purposes of this paper I have called ego-relatedness.
>
> (p. 33)

Ego-relatedness, Winnicott tells us, is a term he is using to refer to a particular aspect of "the relationship of the infant to the mother" (p. 33). "I attach great importance to this relationship, as I consider that it is the stuff out of which friendship is made. It may turn out to be the *matrix of transference*" (p. 33, italics in original).

I think of friendship, in part, in terms of childhood play experience. In my experience with my granddaughters, these girls are interested in rolling me up in a carpet (simulating birth?) and assigning roles (mother, father, son, daughter, schoolteacher) for us to play parents who are talking to one another or talking to teachers or taking care of babies. This might be envisioned in terms of sublimated sexual feelings, but that is not what it feels like to me when playing with my granddaughters, and not what Winnicott has in mind as ego-relatedness, which is to be differentiated from "id-relationships" (p. 34), that is, love relationships, "either crude or in sublimated form" (p. 31). Ego-relatedness is a term that refers to the experience of playing, which involves being by oneself or with others engaged in activities in which they are imaginatively sorting out deeply felt feelings, ideas, and difficulties. Ego-relatedness is not an experience of sexual excitement or desire; it is the form of relatedness underlying playing alone or with someone else.

By contrast, "id-relatedness" is more instinct-bound and has to do with relating to another person with sexual aliveness that is either manifest or sublimated. Such a relationship does not involve the paradoxical relatedness associated with the capacity to be alone. In id-relatedness, one is drawn libidinally to someone else who is a real and separate person. Winnicott adds that the experience of ego-relatedness allows id-impulses to be experienced as real and personal and one's own. This addendum is critical to the narrative Winnicott is developing. Love relationships feel real and personal only because they are built upon a foundation of ego-relatedness, a foundation in which one has experienced being alone in the presence of the mother and carries that experience into the way one experiences one's sexual desire and one's love relationships.

It intrigues me that Winnicott says that ego-relatedness may be the *"matrix of transference."* Winnicott mentions this idea without providing explanation or detail. Perhaps he is suggesting that ego-relatedness is the matrix of transference in the sense that, in the analytic setting, both patient and analyst are alone in the presence of the other. In such a state, the patient and analyst dream their dreams/reveries alone while with someone else (one another). Ego-relatedness may be a "matrix" (Latin for "womb"), an envelope or frame, in which transference experience is generated (imaginative experience in which the present is in the past and the past in the present). Moreover, analytic relatedness is not inherently a love relationship, a relationship inherently sexual in nature. When the analytic relationship includes sexual excitement and desire, it is personal when built upon ego-relatedness. Otherwise, the id-relationship feels out of the patient's control or generic or perverse.

Late in the paper, Winnicott further clarifies the distinction between ego-relatedness and id-relatedness. When describing children's experience of playing, he writes, "we leave out something vital if we do not remember that the play of a child is not happy when complicated by bodily excitements and their physical climaxes" (p. 35). Children's play, in health, is a form of ego-relatedness. The disruption of a child's experience of playing by erotic excitement is an instance in which frightening, uncontained impulse *happens to the child* and disrupts the child's playing.

In the background of Winnicott's paradoxical understanding of the capacity to be alone is still another contribution that he is making to psychoanalytic thinking. Psychoanalysis, as developed by Freud, Ferenczi, Klein, Balint, Fairbairn, Bion, and others, is based on the assumption that there is an internal world and an external world. Who could object to this idea? What else is there but an internal world and an external world? Winnicott objects to the idea. For him, there is a third realm of experience. "This third area of playing [and all other creative activities, including the analytic experience] is not inner psychic reality. It is outside the individual, but it is not the external world" (1971c, p. 51). That realm of experience is not located anywhere. It is not "between" the internal world and the external world, nor does it exist "between" reality and fantasy.

In terms of the capacity to be alone, the third realm of experience is created by the paradoxical tension between the experience of being alone and the experience of being with another person. The paradox involves the individual's being in two places at once: being alone and being in the presence of someone else. This is the third realm in which we live, a world in which we imaginatively come to life, experience our feelings as real and personal, and engage in playing and every other creative activity.

Ego-living

Winnicott returns to the idea that "it will be generally agreed that id-impulse is significant only if it is contained in ego-living" (p. 33). An id-impulse (for example, bodily sexual desire for an external object) is of value to the individual only to the extent that it is experienced in the context of feeling one is a person whose libidinal experience feels alive and real and one's own.

Winnicott continues, "An id-impulse either disrupts a weak ego or else strengthens a strong one" (p. 33). An id-impulse disintegrates a fragile self-organization while it strengthens a strong self-organization. In the latter case, the individual has established a sense of self in which one's desires feel personal and real, which allows one to experience sexual desire as an enrichment of who one is and who one is becoming. So,

id-relationships strengthen the ego when they occur in a framework of ego-relatedness. If this is accepted, then an understanding of the capacity to be alone follows. It is only when alone (that is to say, in the presence of someone) that the infant can discover his own personal life.

(p. 34, italics in original)

Discovering one's own "personal life" occurs in the analytic setting where the patient is alone (with his or her own thoughts, feelings, dreams, and sensations) *and* with the analyst (as the person external to the patient who ends the session). The structure of the analytic setting—the patient lying on the couch with the analyst out of sight behind the couch—facilitates the creation of the paradoxical state of being alone in the presence of someone else.

Relaxing

The infant, when alone (in the presence of the mother), is able to engage in what in adult terms is called "relaxing" (p. 34). The infant in this state is

able to become unintegrated, to flounder, to be in a state in which there is no orientation, to be able to exist for a time without being either a reactor to an external impingement or an active person with a direction of interest or movement.

(p. 34)

I am again reminded of Winnicott's 1952 diagram in which the baby is represented as the circle within an outer circle representing the mother. In that state of isolation (relaxing), the infant is free of the need to be responsive to stimuli from without and stimuli from within; he or she is free to be directionless, unmotivated, and unintegrated. Only under such circumstances is the infant able to create "his own personal life" (p. 34) and is ready for an id experience. "In the course of time there arrives a sensation or an impulse. In this setting the sensation or impulse will feel real and be truly a personal experience" (p. 34).

Here, again, Winnicott makes use of terms and ideas—such as "his own personal life" and impulses that "feel real" and are "truly a personal experience"—that are not part of the register of feelings with which Freud and Klein were concerned.

The object waiting

Winnicott now views, from a different perspective, the role of the object in the capacity to be alone:

It will now be seen why it is important that there is someone available, someone present, although present without making demands; the impulse having arrived, the id experience can be fruitful, and the object can be a part or the whole of the attendant person, namely the mother.

(p. 34)

Part of the role of the mother in the infant's experience of being alone is to be unobtrusively present while she waits for the infant to become ready for his own id-experience (desire) in relation to her. When the infant becomes able to experience his desire as his own (ego-relatedness), a qualitatively new area of experiencing opens to him. The mother, who has been present but unobtrusive, now becomes an object of the infant's desire. What good fortune it is for the infant that his mother has been there (invisibly, unobtrusively) all along so she can now be discovered as an object of his desire!

When the impulse arises, "the id experience can be fruitful" for the infant. The word *fruitful* serves as a metaphor for the ripening of grapes on the vine or the fruit on the tree, the manifestation of the outcome of a natural sexual act of creation.

> It is only under these circumstances that the infant can have an experience which feels real. A large number of such experiences form the basis for a life that has reality in it instead of futility.
>
> (p. 34)

The capacity to be alone underlies our capacity to have lives that feel alive and impulses that feel real and our own.

> The individual who has developed the capacity to be alone is constantly able to rediscover the personal impulse, and the personal impulse is not wasted because the state of being alone is something which (though paradoxically) always implies that someone else is there.
>
> (p. 34)

A person who can be alone (in the presence of someone) is able to repeatedly "rediscover" what it is to have a personal life as one experiences one's own sensations and impulses (one's own desires). And these impulses are "not wasted" because someone else is there waiting to be the object of the id-impulses when they arrive.

Winnicott completes the story of the capacity to be alone by revisiting a topic he discussed earlier:

> In the course of time the individual is able to forgo the *actual* presence of the mother or mother-figure. This has been referred to in such terms as the establishment of an "internal environment."
>
> (p. 34, italics in original)

One must again write Winnicott here. Implicit, it seems to me, is the idea that the infant reaches a point where the actual mother need not (unobtrusively) be there with the infant; instead, the mother becomes "built into the individual's personality, so that there develops a capacity actually to be alone" (p. 36). To my mind, the phrase "actually to be alone" should not be read as indicating that the individual outgrows the paradoxical experience of being alone in the presence of the external object mother. The actual mother is re-placed by the experience of "'an internal environment" as the "someone else" (the external object) in the paradoxical capacity to be alone. The "internal environment" is to be distinguished from the mother as internal object, for to view the mother as an internal object is to collapse the paradox underlying the capacity to be alone.

Concluding comment

As I mentioned at the outset, this is a difficult paper. The difficulty arises in part because paradox is difficult to hold in mind without resolving it. But that is not the entirety of what makes this paper difficult. Additional difficulty arises when Winnicott tries to justify paradoxical thinking and linear thinking. It seems to me to be a stretch to say that "an internal environment" comes to play the role of the external object mother in the capacity to be alone. As I try to picture that situation, I am again drawn to Winnicott's 1952 diagram of the infant within the environment of the mother. But I realize as I do this that nothing could be more linear (unparadoxical) than that diagram.

I do not have an answer to the question Winnicott raises: Does there come a time when the infant entirely takes over the role of the external object mother ("the *actual* presence of the mother") in the paradoxical experience in which the infant is alone and the infant is with the mother? Perhaps the problem may lie in the way in which time is being conceived. It seems to me that when Winnicott says, "In the course of time," he is applying a linear, sequential conception of time ("diachronic time" [Ogden, 2024]) to the para-dox of the capacity to be alone. Perhaps what is required is a "synchronic" conception of time (Ogden, 2024), a conception of time in which all time is experienced in the present moment. The past is gone: this is true of the events that occurred 10 seconds ago and 10 years ago. But in a synchronic experi-ence of time, all that exists is the present moment. The present moment is "the present moment of the past" (Eliot, 1919, p. 11).

The past is part of the present through the impressions that past experience leaves on the individual. "The past is not dead, it is not even past" (Faulkner, 1951). Conceiving of time as synchronic time in relation to the paradox of the capacity to be alone allows the idea of "the course of time" to become closer to the experience of time in playing and dreaming. We do not ask a patient, "How long did that dream last?" or "How long were you playing with that toy?"

From the perspective of synchronic time, one would not have to say that the internal environment comes to play the role once played by the external object mother. Instead, one could conceive of the individual's past experi-ence of the mother as external object as an impression left on the infant that becomes part of who the infant is (not as an internal object). The concepts of an internal and an external world need not be invoked; instead, one is think-ing about past and present experience in relation to who the infant is and is becoming. This way of conceiving of the situation seems more in keeping with the direction Winnicott's thinking takes during the remaining years of his life.

Note

1 This discussion of "The capacity to be alone" is the fifteenth in a series of essays in which I offer "creative readings" of seminal analytic contributions. I have previously discussed works by Freud, Winnicott, Isaacs, Fairbairn, Bion, Loewald, and Searles (Ogden, 2001, 2002, 2004, 2006, 2007a, 2007b, 2010, 2011, 2014, 2015, 2016, 2018, 2021, 2023).

References

Eliot, T. S. (1919). Tradition and individual talent. In *Selected Essays*. New York: Harcourt, Brace, and World, 1960, pp. 3–11.

Faulkner, W. (1951). *Requiem for a Nun*. New York: Random House.

Ogden, T. H. (2024). Rethinking the concepts of the unconscious and analytic time. *Int. J. Psychoanal.* 104, 275–291.

Winnicott, D. W. (1952). Psychoses and child care. In *Through Paediatrics to Psycho-Analysis*. New York: Basic Books, 1975, pp. 219–228.

Winnicott, D. W. (1953). Transitional objects and transitional phenomena. In *Through Paediatrics to Psycho-Analysis*. New York: Basic Books, 1975, pp. 229–242.

Winnicott, D. W. (1958). The capacity to be alone. In *The Maturational Processes and the Facilitating Environment*. New York: International Universities Press, 1965, pp. 29–36.

Winnicott, D. W. (1971a). Transitional objects and transitional phenomena. In *Playing and Reality*. New York: Basic Books, pp. 1–25.

Winnicott, D. W. (1971b). Introduction. In *Playing and Reality*. New York: Basic Books, pp. xi–xiii.

Winnicott, D. W. (1971c). Playing: A theoretical statement. In *Playing and Reality*. New York: Basic Books, pp. 38–52.

9   A letter to a young writer

Dear Fellow Writer,

In response to your letter, I can offer you some thoughts about writing with which you might create something of your own. I do so with some trepidation because I worry that you will take what I say as instruction concerning how you should write instead of reflections on my own experience of writing.

What has been most important to me in my efforts to write is the knowledge that I cannot write like anybody else and no one else can write the way I do. To try to write like someone else is to destroy what is unique to my own experience, my way of talking, my way of thinking, my way of writing, my way of being. Knowing this with certainty has been indispensable to me as a writer.

Being a writer is not a part-time undertaking. I think about writing all the time: when taking a shower, when driving to work, when eating lunch, when waiting in line at a movie theater, when seated in an airplane, when falling asleep. There isn't a moment, day or night, when I am not in some way thinking about writing. Writing isn't what I do, it is who I am. The first question Borges needed answered after his dozen days of septic coma was: "Am I still able to write?" For being a writer was who Borges was. In his attempt to prove to himself that he was still able to write, Borges posed for himself the challenge of writing in a genre in which he had never been able to write: the short story. Borges, in this effort to determine if he was still the writer he was, did not simply write a short story, he invented a new genre of short story. He wrote "Pierre Menard, author of the Quixote" (1939), the first of his astonishing *ficciones*.

Camus (1943) describes the importance of one's dedication to the task of writing: "Works of art are not born in flashes of inspiration but in a daily fidelity" (p. 218). To persist in writing when one feels unable to write is an act of courage. Philip Roth, when suffering from writer's block, spent weeks at a time in his study trying to detect his pulse as a writer. Franz Kafka (1915) wrote in his Diary: "*[11 March]* How time flies; another ten days and I have achieved nothing. It doesn't come off. A page now and then is successful, but I can't keep it up, the next day I am powerless" (p. 332). Virginia Woolf (1921) in her diary: "And I ought to be writing *Jacob's Room*; and I can't, and instead

DOI: 10.4324/9781003528821-10

I shall write down the reason why I can't—this diary being a kindly blank-faced old confidante."

And Iris Murdoch (1943): "Do I write? I've written only three poems & no prose in the last year... but at the moment I'm writing nothing nor do I feel the urge to write." I put my soul into writing; writing is an aggressive act in which I dare to take my own bite out of the apple.

I will mention briefly some other thoughts about writers and writing that may hold some value for you as a young writer:

Everyone who takes his or her writing seriously is a writer.

A writer is a person who writes, not a person who publishes.

A young painter does not study with an experienced artist to learn how that artist paints; he studies with the experienced artist to learn how he, himself, paints.

A writer writes to become a better writer.

Essays of every sort, from scientific papers to political manifestos, are art forms, genres of creative writing, that are due the full respect given to other genres of writing.

There is no magic associated with writing; writing is not a gift of the Muses. It is one's own act of independence.

The more natural writing appears, the more work and talent has gone into it.

A piece of writing is never finished. All I can say about a piece of writing after many drafts is that it is as good as I can make it at this moment. I am never satisfied with what I have written. I do not read what I have published because I am reluctant to see how poor the writing is. Alfonso Reyes, a friend of Borges (1984), said that he "published what he had written to avoid spending his life correcting it: one publishes a book in order to leave it behind, one publishes a book in order to forget it."

I read philosophy as a writer and have found Hegel's (1807) allegory of the master and slave to be an expression of one of the most important ways in which writing sustains me. In Hegel's allegory, the slave does everything for the master: he grows the food the master eats, he builds the house in which the master lives, he weaves the clothes the master wears, he constructs the chair on which the master sits. The master does nothing. The upshot of this arrangement is that the slave achieves consciousness, the capacity for self-reflection, the capacity to talk to himself, the capacity to be both subject and object, I and me. The master never achieves consciousness. This is so because the slave sees himself reflected in the things he makes: in the crops he grows, in the house he builds, in the fabrics he weaves, in the chair he constructs. The master never achieves consciousness because he makes nothing and consequently has nothing in which to see himself reflected. So too, the poem the poet writes, the essay the essayist writes, and the novel the novelist writes are mirrors in which the writer sees himself reflected.

I have spent a good deal of my life writing. This is true not only in terms of the number of hours I have spent writing but also in terms of the way every experience I have lived, real and imaginary, has become part of who I am as a writer. I read as a writer, I dream as a writer, I see films as a writer, I teach as a writer. I am the sum of the impressions my lived experience has left on me, and these impressions are the quarry from which I mine the characters and stories and essays and poems I write. This is not to say that I am a step removed as I engage in reading or viewing a film or falling asleep. Quite the opposite. The experiences of reading, dreaming, watching films, working at my profession, talking to my mother, my wife, my children, my grandchildren, and the checkout clerk at the grocery store all become more immediate and intense when I am at the same time experiencing these activities in all their shifting hues and shades from the perspective of a writer.

As I read, I am cognizant of the structure and length of sentences, the qualities of the voices of the narrator and characters, the way metaphor is used, the way first-person and third-person narration are used, the way music is made in a poem and good prose, and so on. As I read a novel, I am revising the text in my mind as I would revise a draft of my own writing: I rewrite sentences, alter the narrative voice, and consider whether a metaphor works. The authors of books I've read have been my most important teachers of writing.

I maintain my connection with writing as I work in my profession. I am all the time engaged in writing from (not about) the experience I am living as I do my professional work. Without the opportunity to give expression in writing to the thoughts and emotions I experience at work, I think I would lose interest in my profession and perhaps come to resent spending my time doing it. I have learned that it is possible to respond as a writer to experiences while working by transforming these experiences, giving them expression as a detail, a metaphor, a *sotto voce* remark, a turn of plot in what I am writing at the time.

All of us are writers. We write a good deal every day: emails, texts, birthday cards, reminder notes to ourselves. To become a better writer, I take all of my writing seriously, even seemingly trivial sorts of writing. This is nowhere bette illustrated than in William Carlos Williams' "This is just to say" (1934, p. 372).

I have eaten
the plums
that were in
the icebox

and which
you were probably
saving
for breakfast

Forgive me
they were delicious
so sweet
and so cold

I try to keep in mind the way Williams' poem, and many other poems like it, transform the ordinary into art. A written account of one's experience is not always art. Art is what we do with our experience in the act of writing. The possibility of creating art presented itself to me today in the form of responding to an email from my wife asking what time I will be finished working; a note from a member of a seminar saying she's ill and won't be attending the seminar today; a brief story my eight-year-old granddaughter sent me; turning down a request for an endorsement of a book; a thought for a short story I jotted down (as I waited in line at the post office) on a ragged piece of paper in my wallet which I keep there for just such occasions. In each of these instances, I tried to write well, to write phrases and sentences with some life to them, sentences free of cliché, sentences that may have a bit of humor or irony and a bit of music to them. It is satisfying to write even a few words that feel sincere and personal and thought-provoking. An imaginative note is a precious gift to give or receive.

I will focus for a moment on the way I read as a writer. I marvel at the way writers create effects in writing, effects that transcend the symbolic meaning of words. I find that the meaning of sentences lies less in the symbolic value of the words and more in the mysterious ways they affect me.

As I read, I ask myself, "How did he or she do that?" How does William Maxwell (1980), in *So Long, See You Tomorrow*, manage to narrate a portion of the book from the point of view of a dog: "The leaves started falling, and the dog could see stars shining in the tops of the trees" (p. 115). For the dog, the stars are not shining *through* the tops of the trees, they are *in* the tops of the trees. And the dog is witness to the change in the boy she loves, a boy whom she knows has lost everything—his home, his horse, the smell of washday, his books, his work clothes, and so much else. "Take all this away and what have you done to him" (p. 113) the dog wonders.

There is a sentence from Eudora Welty's short story, "The Wide Net," which I return to again and again. In this long sentence, Brucie, a six-year-old Black boy in Mississippi in the first quarter of the 20th century, watches his older brother Grady count the cars of a freight train passing in the distance:

> It seemed like a little festival procession, moving with the slowness of ignorance or a dream, from distance to distance, the tiny pink and gray cars like secret boxes, Grady was counting the cars to himself, as if he could certainly see each one clearly, and Brucie watched his lips, hushed and cautious, the way he would watch a bird drinking.
>
> (p. 159)

This sentence is made up of a series of ten descriptive phrases moving along like the cars of a freight train. In the first part of this sentence, the pace of a freight train is likened to the torpor of "ignorance or a dream." The words *ignorance* and *dream* are haunting in the pairing of all that is vacant and all that is possible. The narrator is speaking of a distinctive quality of Southerners: most everything about Southerners seems to move languorously, including their ignorance and their dreams. Welty once commented that because she's a Southerner, she doesn't have to make up anything.

The sentence reaches a crescendo in its final two phrases describing the way Brucie watches his older brother counting: "hushed and cautious, the way he would watch a bird drinking." How better to describe the way this younger brother watches his older brother's lips moving as he counts the cars: "the way he would watch a bird drinking." The music of the words is tender, deriving from the joining of two soft shh-sounds ("hushed" and "cautious") followed by the alliteration of three soft *w* sounds in "the way he would watch." These alliterations were almost certainly unplanned. They "just happen" in the hands of a writer writing well.

In a relatively short sentence by Patrick White in *The Solid Mandala* (1966), the narrator describes Waldo overhearing his mother and younger brother talking: "It was about this time that Waldo decided every member of his family was hopeless but inevitable" (p. 38). The linking of the words *hopeless* and *inevitable* captures a truth about families in that they are hopeless in the sense that they will never be what one wishes they were; in fact, they fail in every respect, and yet one's family feels inevitable, inescapable.

I write notes and page numbers on the inside of the back cover of every novel, and every collection of short stories or poems I read. I do not feel I have read a book if I have not left these notes about a particular word choice, the delicacy of a metaphor, a change in the voice of a character, a long sentence that moves with all the grace of a butterfly unfurling its wings. I should add that I never return to those notes, probably because I am no longer the reader or the writer who read that book.

T. S. Eliot distilled into six words the remarkable statement, "Immature poets imitate, mature poets steal." To say that immature poets imitate is not a dismissal of young poets, for we all begin as immature writers and make our way into writing in part by imitating the voices of the writers that have inspired us. In my own immaturity, I wrote by imitating Melville in *Moby-Dick,* which proved a heavy mantle for a 17-year-old boy to carry.

The "thefts" by mature poets, to my mind, are the lines from other poets' poems one installs word for word into one's own poems (a practice Eliot subscribed to); but more important than that, as one matures as a writer one accrues a background sense that one's writing is a part of a whole to which no individual may lay claim.

It has taken countless experiences in reading, beginning in grade school, to awaken me to the fact that the words on the page are all there is. There is nothing beneath them or behind them. Reading as a writer involves looking into the words, listening to the sounds they make, seeing how the words work together to create wondrous effects. That is the art and the craft of writing.

I am always writing. In the period between completing one piece of writing and beginning the next, I am a person who is preparing to write. When the beginnings of an idea occur to me, I feel that I have somehow had this idea all my life and only now am finding a way to think it, and possibly write it. A friend, who is an artist, tells me when he shows me a new painting, "It has taken 75 years to paint this painting."

From the time I was an adolescent, I have been intrigued with the way words work, how they convey meaning, how they create meaning, and how meaning can be stripped from them. While in high school, after dinner, I began repeating to myself the name given to the piece of cloth in front of me on the table. I decided to see what happened if I repeated the word *napkin* to myself. After 15 or 20 repetitions of the word, the name for the object dissolved into a sound that no longer was a word. The object no longer had a name, it had a sound that could be replaced by any other sound because there was nothing intrinsic to the sound that connected it to the object. I became frightened that every name I had for objects could be reduced to a sound that was impossible to remember. If this were to occur, I would lose my sanity and become unable to speak or even think. This experience revealed to me one of the dark secrets of language: its power to create me and the world in which I live and its power to strip that world of meaning.

I will mention aspects of the way I go about writing both fiction and non-fiction, not as advice concerning how you should write but as a description of the way I write. I try to claim certain hours of the week in which to write without outside interference, but this is not always possible, as was almost always the case when my children were young. When there is no time to put aside for writing, I use scraps of time, seize minutes during the day or night in which to write, for example, the minutes during which my wife was reading a bedtime story to our children, minutes or hours spent waiting to board a train or plane, the minutes waiting for a client or colleague who is late for a meeting.

I avoid reading the work of others on the subject about which I am writing. I have found that if I read what others have written on a subject, I am inclined either to argue with them (which is not interesting for me or the reader) or to surrender to them with the feeling that my ideas have already been written and need not be written again. I am not alone in feeling this way. Winnicott (1945) elegantly states in the opening sentences of an essay:

> I shall not first give an historical survey and show the development of my ideas from the theories of others, because my mind does not work that way. What happens is that I gather this and that, here and there, settle down to clinical experience, form my own theories and then, last of all, interest myself in where I stole what. Perhaps this is as good a method as any.
>
> (p. 145)

Getting out of my own way while writing—refraining from being excessively critical of what I am saying—is both necessary and difficult. I find reviews of my work to be particularly uninstructive for me. I no longer read book reviews because in the decades in which I did read them, I kept the reviewer in my mind as a voice urging me to write in a manner he or she would have me write. This was so regardless of whether the review was laudatory or damning. Neither do I talk with anyone about what I am writing, for there too, an enthusiastic response or a critical one lingers as a bias that interferes with my own process of writing. Paul Klee wrote that when he was young, his studio was filled with the artists he most admired, and as he grew older, the room emptied, until finally he was alone as he painted.

I find that one of the most reliable ways of improving a piece of writing is deletion of text: deleting every extra word, extra phrase, extra sentence, extra metaphor, extra character whose presence is not necessary to the movement of the story or essay. I am reminded here of Tom Stoppard's (1999) definition of poetry: "the simultaneous compression of language and expansion of meaning" (p. 10).

I have learned that there are many times when my writing seems to me "unproductive" in that it is not yielding an organization of sentences in which I am creating a structure of thinking or storytelling. But I discover again and again that writing has to be "unproductive"—without shape or direction—before it becomes part of a larger, more defined structure of meaning. The previous ways I have conveyed meaning must give way to new ones if the writing is to feel fresh and original to me.

If I go chasing after an idea or a narrative twist, it eludes me. If I am quiet and simply write, it may come to me. I can imagine a response to what I have just said: "It comes to you because you are an experienced writer, and I'm not. I am a newcomer stalled in the anteroom of writing." I would reply:

> Like everything else one does—driving a car, baking a soufflé, playing tennis—it takes a great deal of practice to do these things well, and even after a great deal of practice, it takes time and patience, and there is no guarantee it will ever come out as you would like it.

I have thrown away essays, short stories, and novels that have died on the vine. Those false starts may not ever come to be parts of my later writing, but they all contribute to my becoming a better writer.

When writing, I persist until I hear the sound of good sentences. I read Melville and Shakespeare in high school. Their writing was "good" because I was told it was good. I had not yet developed an ear for good writing. I first began to be able to hear good sentences—sentences that make sense in their own way—when taking a freshman writing composition course. Halfway through the semester, the professor read a paragraph written by a student in response to the question, "Describe a situation in which you were feeling good." The student described stepping down the front steps of his house, walking down the sidewalk, and saying hello to a dog as he passed by. I was struck by the detail of saying hello to a dog. I was able, for the first time, to hear the sound of good writing.

I find the difference between fiction and nonfiction to be imaginary. All autobiography is fiction, and all fiction is autobiography. Fiction is not a falsification of reality; it is the most reliable medium for the expression of the emotional truth of an experience. Writing dialogue is one of the most fertile ways I have of conveying who a character is at a particular point in a story. As narrator, I could say that the character is diffident or caustic or grandiose, but those qualities are better conveyed by the voice with which the character speaks.

In writing about experiences of any sort, I try to describe, not explain, for I do not have explanations for something as complex and mysterious as human emotion and behavior. Life is not comprehensible; it is not even plausible. When we write, we do not record life; we create life.

References

Borges, J. L. (1939). Pierre Menard, author of the Quixote. In Labyrinths: *Selected Stories and Other* Writings, ed. D. Yates & J. Irby. New York: New Directions, 1964, pp. 36–44.

Borges, J. L. (1984). *Twenty-four Conversations with Borges by Roberto Alifano, 1981– 1983*. New York: Grove Press.

Camus, A. (1943). Intelligence and the scaffold. In *Lyrical and Critical Essays*, ed. P. Thody, trans. E. Kennedy. New York: Vintage Books, 1968, pp. 210–218.

Hegel, G. W. F. (1807). *Hegel's Phenomenology of Spirit*, trans. A. V. Miller. Oxford: Oxford University Press.

Kafka, F. (1915). *Diaries, 1910–1923*, ed. M. Brod. New York: Schocken Books, 1948.

Maxwell, W. (1980). *So Long, See You Tomorrow*. New York: Vintage.

Murdoch, I. (1943). Letter to Frank Thompson. In *Writer at War: Letters and Diaries, 1939–1945*. London: Short Books, Ltd., 2000.

Stoppard. T. (1999). Pragmatic theater. *New York Rev. Books*, September 23, 1999, pp. 8–10.

Welty, E. (1942). The wide net. In *The Collected Stories of Eudora Welty*. New York: Mariner Books, 1955, pp. 153–170.

White, P. (1966). *The Solid Mandala*. New York: Penguin.

Williams, W. C. (1934). This is just to say. In *The Collected Poems of William Carlos Williams, 1919–1939*, ed. A. Litz & C. Mac Gowan, Vol. 1. New York: New Directions, 1991, p. 372.

Winnicott, D. W. (1945). Primitive emotional development. In *Through Paediatrics to Psycho-Analysis*, New York: Basic Books, 1975, pp. 145–156.

Woolf, V. (1921). *A Writer's Diary*. New York, Mariner Books Classics, 2003.

Acknowledgments

I would like to thank *The Psychoanalytic Quarterly* for the use of the following papers in this volume:

"Ontological psychoanalysis in clinical practice." *Psychoanalytic Quarterly* 93: 13–31, 2024. © *The Psychoanalytic Quarterly*.

"Giving back what the patient brings: On Winnicott's 'Mirror-role of mother and family in child development.' *Psychoanalytic Quarterly* 93: 413–430, 2024. © *The Psychoanalytic Quarterly*.

I would like to thank the *International Journal of Psychoanalysis* for the use of the following papers in this volume:

"Rethinking the concepts of the unconscious and analytic time." *International Journal of Psychoanalysis* 105: 275–291, 2024. © The Institute of Psychoanalysis.

"Like the belly of a bird breathing: On Winnicott's 'Mind in relation to the psyche-soma.'" *International Journal of Psychoanalysis* 101: 7–22, 2023. © The Institute of Psychoanalysis.

"What Alive Means: On Winnicott's 'Transitional Objects and Transitional Phenomena.'" *International Journal of Psychoanalysis* 101: 837–856. © The Institute of Psychoanalysis.

I would like to thank the *Journal of the American Psychoanalytic Association* for the use of the following paper in this volume:

"Transformations at the dawn of verbal language." *Journal of the American Psychoanalytic Association*, 2024. © The American Psychoanalytic Association.

I would like to thank the *Parapraxis* for the use of the following paper in this volume:

"A letter to a young writer." *Parapraxis,* Summer, 182–187, 2024. © *Parapraxis*.

I would like to thank New Directions Publishing and Alliance House for the use of the following poem by William Carlos Williams in this volume:

"This is just to say." William Carlos Williams from *The Collected Poems: Volume I, 1909–1939*, copyright © 1938 by New Directions Publishing Corp. Reprinted by permission of New Directions Publishing Corp. and Alliance House.

I would like to thank Gina Atkinson and Terri Smith for their help with the production phase of this book and Patricia Marra for the fine index she created.

I would also like to express my profound gratitude to my wife, Sandra Ogden, for her thoughtful editing of this book.

Index

Note: Page numbers followed by "n" denote endnotes.

For Product Safety Concerns and Information please contact our EU
representative GPSR@taylorandfrancis.com
Taylor & Francis Verlag GmbH, Kaufingerstraße 24, 80331 München, Germany

www.ingramcontent.com/pod-product-compliance
Lightning Source LLC
Chambersburg PA
CBHW052012270326
41929CB00015B/2890